D1294565

Marcel Proust and His Literary Friends

Marcel Proust and His Literary Friends

LAURENT LESAGE

ILLINOIS STUDIES IN LANGUAGE AND LITERATURE: *Vol. 45*

THE UNIVERSITY OF ILLINOIS PRESS
URBANA, 1958

MANUFACTURED IN THE UNITED STATES OF AMERICA.
LIBRARY OF CONGRESS CATALOG CARD NO. 57-6952.

Acknowledgments

I should like here to express my gratitude to two professors of French literature at the University of Illinois: Paul-Emile Jacob, who, when I was his pupil, first kindled my interest in Proust and generously approved for a master's degree my rudimentary study of Proust as a literary critic; Philip Kolb, whose monumental index of Proust's correspondence was an indispensable tool and guide in the preparation of the chapters that follow.

Three portions have already appeared in periodicals, namely:

"Proust and Gide, Lifelong Antagonists," *Modern Language Journal*, XXXVI (April, 1952), 159-65.

"Proust and Henri de Régnier," *Modern Language Notes*, LXVIII (January, 1953), 8-13.

"Marcel Proust's Professor of Beauty: Robert de Montesquiou," *The American Society of the French Legion of Honor Magazine*, XXVII (Spring, 1956), 65-76.

Contents

Introduction

Il n'y a peut-être pas de jours de notre enfance que nous ayons si pleinement vécus que ceux que nous avons cru laisser sans les vivre, ceux que nous avons passés avec un livre préféré.[1]

At Illiers by the hawthorn hedge, in Auteuil at Uncle Weil's, the boy Marcel spent his summer holidays in precocious indulgence of "ce vice impuni, la lecture." Like young Rousseau, he devoured novels and romances, losing himself completely in the life they represented. Gautier, Hugo, Dickens, Eliot, Balzac were his favorite companions of the long, warm afternoons. His universe was bounded by the covers of a book. Therein seemed to him his real life and his greatest happiness. The fragile, sensitive child, preferring solitary reading to participation in the games of his classmates, would gradually grow into the invalid shut-in; he would always remain a stranger to the activities and pursuits that constitute the lives of the majority of humanity: "Ses voyages dans les bibliothèques auront été les seuls qu'ait faits ce sédentaire, qui courait la prétentaine avec les prosateurs, les poètes, les hommes de science." [2]

Proust chose to read about life rather than live it, but who can say that his pleasures were therefore less exciting or his sorrows less authentic? Jean Santeuil is far from convinced when he hears Rustinlor, the poet who has forsaken verse for life, boast that in so doing he has "left the shadow for the prey." [3] The personages of literature were for Proust no less real than actual persons. In his own writing the living and the dead, characters from novels and creatures of his own imagination, all dwell happily together. His confusion was, to be sure, usually a conscious one, although there are times when it appears actually paranoiac.

Literature served Proust as a touchstone. A situation, an event, a personality became comprehensible to him when he had located in the vast storehouses of his memory its fictional counterpart. Such a person is so much like the Duchesse de Langeais, he would say. Everyone or everything he met in real life possessed its model or prototype in the literary microcosm. In interpreting his experience he called upon literature as the reference nearest at hand. It is no wonder that the line of demarcation between life and literature became at times dangerously indistinct.

[1] Proust, *Pastiches et mélanges* (Gallimard, 1919), p. 225.
[2] Jacques-Emile Blanche, *Mes Modèles* (Stock, 1928), p. 139.
[3] Proust, *Jean Santeuil* (Gallimard, 1952), II, 30.

One of those old-fashioned albums in which people used to ask their friends to record their sentiments gives us a revealing picture of Proust at the age of thirteen. To answer "votre occupation préférée?" Marcel wrote in: "la lecture, la rêverie, les vers."[4] Surrounded by a cultivated family, with mother and grandmother fervent readers of French classics, the boy read to his heart's content. They inculcated in him a particular devotion to Baudelaire, La Bruyère, Mme de Sévigné, Musset, and Sand. Among the English, he admired Dickens, Thomas Hardy, Stevenson, and George Eliot. *The Thousand and One Nights,* too, was a very dear favorite.

At the Lycée Condorcet, where Proust took his schooling, considerable emphasis was laid upon literature. There Proust met young men of good family who shared his interest in literature and who also would one day make their own mark in letters. Daniel Halévy, Fernand Gregh, Jacques Bizet, Robert de Flers, Jacques Baignières, Robert Dreyfus, Louis de la Salle, Marcel Boulenger, and Gabriel Trarieux were among his daily companions. Toward 1888 they developed into a little coterie, and would meet before and after classes to discuss the writers of the day. They were ardent partisans of the moderns: Barrès, France, Lemaître, Maeterlinck. To their way of thinking, some of the professors at even a school with as up-to-date leanings in literature as Condorcet were too old-fashioned. They gleefully ridiculed those who did not show proper admiration for Léon Dierx and Leconte de Lisle. The letters young Proust wrote at the time bear a strong perfume of the latter's grandiloquent manner. Love of literature prompted these schoolboys to found several reviews of ephemeral existence. One of them was the *Revue Verte,* copied by hand and passed to the subscribers; another, mimeographed, the *Revue Lilas.* In them one may observe Proust's first literary efforts. Under the able guidance of Maxime Gaucher, who was at the time literary critic for the *Revue Bleue,* Proust was already manifesting a critical talent. His themes and dissertations show remarkable maturity and prophesy the master he would become.

In exchanging for his lycée cap the top hat of a fashionable young man about town, Proust did not renounce his keen interest in literature or break all ties with his companions of the schoolyard. In society, he sought out persons associated with the arts: painters, musicians, and particularly writers. The dinner parties that Proust attended were graced by the presence of such writers of the day as Bourget, Brochard, Vogüé, Maupassant, Porto-Riche, Hervieu, Hermant, Vandérem. What an exciting transition it was for him to move from the world of books into the world

[4] From the album of Antoinette Félix-Faure. See André Maurois, *À La Recherche de Marcel Proust* (Hachette, 1949), p. 18.

of their authors! At Mme de Caillavet's he could meet Anatole France; at Mme Lemaire's, Robert de Montesquiou. He became the intimate friend of several writers' sons. When his father wished him to prepare for diplomacy Proust dutifully went to the École des Sciences politiques, but without conviction. Everything except literature and philosophy seemed to him "a waste of time." [5] When his Condorcet friends, although now widely dispersed in various schools or professions, came together once again to found another review, this one to be called *Le Banquet,* Proust saw in it a means of furthering his literary career and enthusiastically collaborated in the venture.

We can see already from Proust's early articles that he was a great reader. Several of the great and many of the lesser authors of our times have assumed the pose that their writing is free from influence, that their art has not been sullied by contact with libraries. Not so Proust, who believed that the Muses are daughters of Memory and that no art is possible without remembrance. He declared that translation, the most intimate contact that can be established between one writer and another, is the best training for a literary career: "Il n'y a pas de meilleure manière d'arriver à prendre conscience de ce qu'on sent soi-même que d'essayer de recréer en soi ce qu'a senti un maître. Dans cet effort profond c'est notre pensée elle-même que nous mettons, avec la sienne, au jour." [6] In the dark, mahogany dining room of the apartment in the rue de Courcelles, where the Prousts had moved in 1900, Marcel set himself to translating Ruskin, a task that he pursued for five or six years. There also he read late into the night favorite French authors—Saint-Simon, Chateaubriand, Sainte-Beuve—and tried to imitate their style of writing. There is no greater evidence of the intimate communion Proust enjoyed with writers than the pastiches that he dedicated to them.

Whether in specific essays, or embedded in the epic narrative of *À La Recherche du temps perdu,* we come frequently upon the topic of literature. Particularly in *Le Temps retrouvé* there are huge sections entirely expository in nature. Jacques-Emile Blanche comments: "Dans son œuvre gigantesque, ciselée, laquée, comme un cabinet chinois aux tiroirs secrets, on trouverait épars de quoi faire des volumes d'articles par le plus original des critiques littéraires." [7] Literature invades the fictional parts, too, where it serves in several interesting ways. A scene may be presented in the frame of a literary reference. Claude-Edmonde Magny remarks that Proust presents the Verdurin salon through a sort of Goncourt pastiche: "Il est d'ailleurs remarquable que ce ne soit pas par les yeux d'un de ses

[5] From an unpublished letter of Proust to his father. See *ibid.*, p. 52.
[6] *Pastiches et mélanges,* pp. 195-96.
[7] Blanche, p. 139.

propres personnages, Charlus, Morel ou Albertine, que Proust cherche à voir le salon Verdurin, mais à travers les Goncourt, comme si cet observatoire tout construit qu'offre la littérature lui était indispensable pour percevoir le monde." [8] A literary reference may be used to delineate character. Personages reveal themselves through their literary opinions, and since much of Proust's dialogue is salon conversation, the technique seems quite a natural one. In some cases reference becomes something of a personal symbol or motif, as for example the repeated allusions to Balzac used to situate Charlus in characteristic attitudes.

In the great symphony of Proust's works, literary motifs continually recur. The mixture of critical and creative elements in *À La Recherche du temps perdu* has troubled many commentators on Proust who think of them as products of distinct or even diametrically opposed activities. They need not be, and on this evidence alone one cannot prove that parts of Proust's novel were later interpolations. Such a mingling is fundamental in all Proust's writing; he seemed to feel the creative urge and the critical urge simultaneously. Therefore much of his criticism took an indirect form. We observe his concern over how he should present his Sainte-Beuve article. A conventional article would not do it—it should be rather a conversation: " La deuxième commence par un récit du matin, du réveil. Maman vient me voir près de mon lit, je lui dis que j'ai l'idée d'une étude sur Sainte-Beuve, je la lui soumets et la lui développe." [9] The novelist and the critic met in Proust. He created characters by means of criticism, and presented criticism by means of characters.

Proust's ability to fuse himself with another author reached its highest expression in the pastiche, an art somewhere between translation and conventional criticism. His self-effacement and acceptance of discipline inclined him to this sort of literary exercise. His close reading and gifts of memory and mimicry made possible an imitation so remarkably exact that the model seems actually to be speaking. Proust called his pastiches synthetic criticism. They illustrate once again that Proust's creative instinct was so strong that he sought always to present his criticism in an indirect form.

Friends testify to what we know already from his writings, that Proust's comments on an author were never doctrinaire nor didactic, never deformed by erudition. Far different from the methods of Taine and Sainte-Beuve, his approach amounted to an intimate communion. In his criticism, as in his pastiches, his own personality was so fluid that it seemed to melt into that of the subject. Jacques Porel says that when Proust talked about a book he *became* its hero:

[8] Magny, *Histoire du romain français* (Ed. du Seuil, 1950), I, 188.

[9] Proust, *Le Balzac de Monsieur de Guermantes* (Ides et Calendes, 1950), p. 15. Cf. *Correspondance générale* (Plon, 1931), II, 45.

N'ayant aucune prudence littéraire, il s'entretenait familièrement avec tous les chefs-d'œuvre. Ce qu'il vous disait était intime et savoureux. C'était le fruit d'un long commerce avec les grands écrivains. Il les connaissait bien, et n'en avait pas peur. C'étaient ceux-là ses vrais amis. Il vous parlait d'eux comme il venait de le faire de vous-même. Il n'y avait plus de trônes, plus de privilèges. Tout le monde se promenait dans les rues, bras-dessus, bras-dessous.
Le mot culture ne convenait pas à Proust. Il avait une immense connaissance de tout. Impossible d'être moins didactique, moins prévu dans ses observations. Impossible aussi de vous intéresser davantage à la personne ou à l'œuvre d'un grand homme. Proust savait tout mais son point de vue n'avait subi aucune des déformations de l'érudition. Il était simple comme un innocent ou prétendait l'être. Quand il parlait de Muichkine de *L'Idiot,* il devenait le héros lui-même. Cela lui faisait tenir constamment des propos pleins d'originalité sur des sujets rebattus. . . .

Proust frequently talked to Porel about Balzac:

J'ai écouté bien des fanatiques de Balzac, mon père, les frères Daudet, Pierre Benoit. D'autres encore. Aucun n'avait la manière de Proust. Encore une fois, nul didactisme. Mais l'impression qu'on allait retrouver Balzac lui-même, qu'il allait sûrement venir, s'asseoir à notre table. N'est-ce pas cela, *connaître* un auteur? . . . Cette soirée fit plus que tout le reste pour me ramener à Balzac, me le faire relire avec passion.[10]

M. Porel's testimony is proof of the charm and persuasion of Proust's critical methods. We are not privileged to sit by his bedside listening to him discourse on his reading, but when his pen wanders in the direction of literature, in his letters and his works, we have the impression of a causerie, sometimes playful or precious, sometimes gravely inspired or rhapsodical, by a gentleman of exquisite culture and sensitivity.

As in a real chat, we cannot expect to find purely objective evaluations in Proust's incidental remarks. Much of our information regarding his opinions comes from letters never meant for publication. He warns us not to take them too literally: "Ce qui nous fait trembler en pensant à ce que croiront de nos idées littéraires ceux qui plus tard retrouveront certains articles, ou, si notre correspondance était publiée, liraient certaines lettres." [11] Only by carefully studying concomitant factors and comparing one statement with one found elsewhere can we hope to arrive at Proust's unbiased thought. Most of all, we must take into account traits of Proust's character likely to color his judgments. "Un des écrivains pour qui j'ai la plus profonde admiration" is a qualifier that Proust lavishes on all sorts of second-rate authors. It is impossible to interpret such praise as anything other than politeness. His adverse criticism, comparatively rare, is often oblique, hedged, for example, by

[10] Porel, " Marcel Proust chez Réjane," *La Table Ronde,* October, 1950, pp. 86-91.
[11] *Jean Santeuil,* II, 250-51.

anxious regard for his correspondent's feelings: "Enfin, je ne veux pas aborder le sujet Moréas, sur lequel vous ne pensez probablement pas comme moi qui ne l'admire presque pas (si, un peu, mais pas énormément, même très peu)." [12] Modesty, flattery, sincerity—all are pulling in different directions. He flatters and he claws: "Il sera un peu trop poli, un peu trop complimenteur, et comme ses flatteries seront, en fait, une réaction de défense ou de protection, il réagira, dans le secret de ses *Carnets* et *Cahiers,* par une critique impitoyable, de sorte qu'un excès de tendresse pourra, par une curieuse transmutation, chez lui se changer en cruauté." [13]

What Proust has to say about writers tells us much about himself, and we are always eager to gain new insights into this strange, but yet so human, genius. What he has to say about writers sends us back to them with new and provoking ideas. We can even pretend a little, forget for a moment our attitudes of the mid-twentieth century grimly turned toward significance and social consciousness, to view some old-fashioned authors through the glass of their great contemporary who saw them and chatted with them in drawing rooms of the aristocrats and *haute bourgeoisie* in the fabulous Paris of the early 1900's.

[12] *Correspondance générale,* II, 98.
[13] Maurois, p. 24.

CHAPTER ONE

Dear Friends and Masters

Anatole France

Il est probable que l'image d'Anatole France a beaucoup compté pour Proust à ses débuts.[1]

When Proust was twenty, his favorite prose writers were Anatole France and Pierre Loti. Other than a few references to the fact that he was reading the author of *Pêcheur d'Islande* and recommending him warmly to his mother, Proust makes little mention of Loti. Anatole France, on the contrary, figures prominently in Proust's letters and serves as a prototype for Bergotte in *À La Recherche du temps perdu.*[2] Throughout the 1880's France's reputation had been steadily growing. *Le Crime de Sylvestre Bonnard* and *Le Livre de mon ami* were enthusiastically received and commented upon by all those who kept abreast of the new writing. Marcel Proust and his classmates at Condorcet considered France an exciting modern. They eagerly followed his newspaper articles, pondered his opinions and judgments in literature. Shortly before Proust's twentieth birthday, *Thaïs* came out, and its wide popularity was making France an author very much in vogue.

It is generally accepted that Proust is recalling his own experience with France when, in *À La Recherche du temps perdu,* he describes his hero's first contacts with Bergotte's writings. Bloch has told young Marcel about the new writer Bergotte, adding in his affected schoolboy language that Leconte de Lisle, the "Delphic oracle," holds Bergotte in high esteem: "Lis donc ces proses lyriques, et si le gigantesque assembleur de rythmes qui a écrit *Baghavat* et le *Levrier de Magnus* a dit vrai, par Apollon tu goûteras . . . les joies nectaréennes de l'Olympos."[3] We know that

[1] Pierre Abraham, *Proust* (Rieder, 1930), p. 49.

[2] "Innombrables sont les lecteurs qui dans le Bergotte des premiers volumes, ou plutôt dans les œuvres de Bergotte telles que Proust les décrit, veulent trouver un reflet d'Anatole France ou un mélange d'Anatole France et de Bergson." *Ibid.*, p. 49.

[3] *Du Côté de chez Swann* (Gallimard, 1919), I, 126. (The edition of *À La Recherche du temps perdu* utilized throughout is the 1949 printing.) The poet Rustinlor of *Jean Santeuil,* who, with Claudius Xelnor, prefigures Bloch, makes an exception of France in his sweeping dismissal of Jean's enthusiasm among the poets: "Tandis que les scélérats que vous avez la faiblesse d'aimer, Weiss, Lemaître et ce France qui est pourtant un assez subtil coco, tous ces gens intelligents ou qui semblent faire les

France began his career under the patronage of the "gigantesque assembleur de rythmes." This reference to Leconte de Lisle's patronage and the allusion to rhythmic prose suggest, from the first reference to Bergotte, that Proust has France in mind.

From the analysis of Marcel's reactions to a book by Bergotte, we infer what in France appealed to the young Proust. The secret of his charm lies first in his style. Marcel speaks of a "flot caché d'harmonie," "flux mélodique," "effusion musicale." Then of "les expressions rares, presque archaïques qu'il aimait employer à certains moments." In sad passages, "une certaine brusquerie, un accent presque rauque." The studied elegance and harmony of France's prose, its delicate mannerisms, are not lost upon Proust's sensitive ear. Already we find intimations of Proust's theory of the function of the artist: "Chaque fois qu'il parlait de quelque chose dont la beauté m'était restée jusque-là cachée, des forêts de pins, de la grêle, de *Notre Dame de Paris,* d'*Athalie* ou de *Phèdre,* il faisait dans une image exploser cette beauté jusqu'à moi." [4] Enchanted with the new spectacles that this writer offers him to view the world, Proust begs for the master's viewpoint on everything in the universe.

He recognizes in Bergotte an irony akin to his own: "Un jour, ayant rencontré dans un livre de Bergotte, à propos d'une vieille servante, une plaisanterie que le magnifique et solennel langage de l'écrivain rendait encore plus ironique, mais qui était la même que j'avais si souvent faite à ma grand'mère en parlant de Françoise. . . ." [5] In *Temps perdu,* Proust will show himself to be as great an ironist as France himself. Through phrases that captivate the boy, Bergotte teaches him lessons in "idealistic" philosophy which recalls the skepticism of a generation nourished by Schopenhauer ("vain songe de la vie," "l'inépuisable torrent des belles apparences," "tourment stérile et délicieux de comprendre et d'aimer"), and which prefigures what Proust will illustrate in his novel. Bergotte's work expresses "toute une philosophie nouvelle . . . par de merveilleuses images." [6] Anatole France did not describe his work in other terms: "un manuel élémentaire de philosophie et de morale, accompagné d'images." [7]

To this philosophy Marcel swore lifelong adherence. He looked forward eagerly to the philosophy year at the lycée. Proust reached this class in the year 1888-89, the period André Maurois considers the most important

intelligents sont absolument incapables d'écrire correctement un poème régulier. Quant à un sonnet, je n'en parle pas: excepté France qui n'a pas toujours été damné, ils ne savent même pas ce que c'est." *Jean Santeuil,* I, 127.

[4] *Du Côté de chez Swann,* I, 132-33.

[5] *Ibid.,* p. 134.

[6] *Ibid.,* p. 131.

[7] Jacques Suffel, *Anatole France* (Ed. du Myrte, 1946), pp. 169-70.

one in his intellectual development: "Elle [Bergotte's philosophy] me rendait impatient d'arriver à l'âge où j'entrerais au collège, dans la classe appellée Philosophie. Mais je ne voulais pas qu'on y fît autre chose que vivre uniquement par la pensée de Bergotte, et si l'on m'avait dit que les métaphysiciens auxquels je m'attacherais alors ne lui ressembleraient en rien, j'aurais ressenti le désespoir d'un amoureux qui veut aimer pour la vie et à qui on parle des autres maîtresses qu'il aura plus tard."[8] This passage reveals that by the time of Proust's senior year at the lycée a part of Bergotte's philosophy had lost its message and that the thinkers to whom Darlu, his teacher, was introducing him had become his new gods.[9] At this time Lachelier, Fouillée, and Boutroux were preparing the ground for Bergson. Darlu was echoing the new patterns of thought in his classroom. Darlu referred to Anatole France as a "joli cerveau," and France returned the compliment! Proust listened to his teacher.[10]

Would the years to come further alienate Proust from Bergotte? We shall turn to this matter later. But before his first ardor could cool very much, Proust was to meet France in person. This event intensified his interest, at the same time shifting its basis somewhat.

Before leaving the lycée, Proust was already beginning his remarkable career of young-man-about-town. The following year, 1889, he was isolated weekdays in Orléans, doing his stint in the army. Sundays, however, he was free to pursue his social career in Paris. He often called on Mme Arman de Caillavet, whose son Gaston had become one of Proust's close friends. His encounter with France in the famous drawing room of the avenue Hoche was a fond dream come true. The young man's emotions are recorded in the scene where Marcel is introduced to Bergotte. Like all those whose enthusiasm has created an idealized portrait, Proust was cruelly disappointed when he was brought face to face with the author whom he imagined as a "doux Chantre aux cheveux blancs."[11] The France whom he had "élaboré . . . goutte à goutte, comme une stalactite, avec la transparente beauté de ses livres . . . se trouvait d'un seul coup ne plus pouvoir être d'aucun usage, du moment qu'il fallait conserver le nez en colimaçon et utiliser la barbiche noire."[12]

[8] *Du Côté de chez Swann*, I, 135.

[9] It is interesting to note in this connection a remark by Léon Pierre-Quint that alters the picture somewhat. Not knowing Pierre-Quint's authority, I can only repeat what he says: "Longtemps Marcel Proust s'est passionné pour la métaphysique. Il aimait avec ses amis discuter les grands systèmes. Mais bientôt, quand il devint un fidèle du salon de Mme Arman de Caillavet, Anatole France devait, par son scepticisme, le guérir de cette passion, qui resta malgré tout un peu la sienne jusqu'à la fin de sa vie." *Marcel Proust* (Sagittaire, 1946), p. 437.

[10] See Maurois, *À la Recherche de Marcel Proust*, p. 37.

[11] *À L'Ombre des jeunes filles en fleurs* (Gallimard, 1919), I, 149.

[12] *Ibid.*, p. 150. Such early disillusionments may be partly responsible for Proust's

Proust, whose sensitivity made him keenly aware of the incongruity of an ugly bespectacled professor reading beautiful poetry, would henceforth be obliged to add the unfortunate nose and the goatee to his portrait of the author.

But France's ability to lionize a drawing room was an achievement that compensated for lack of personal beauty, and Proust accordingly paid him persistent court. As an habitué of Mme de Caillavet's "at homes," and later of the Villa Saïd itself, Proust had ample opportunity to see and converse with the author whom he had once revered at a distance. He now moved in the same social circles and for many years maintained contact with France. Dinners, parties, receptions brought the two frequently together. Observing the master at close range, Proust took passionate interest in comparing the social personality of the man with what he appeared to be in his works. One understands his great interest in the chapter of *La Domination* where Anna de Noailles depicts a famous writer at home. The young hero of the novel, Antoine Arnault, has been invited to the master's country home. There he studies the unheroic and somewhat senile individual who contrasts so markedly with the glory of his name: "Ah, me dis-je, voici donc cet homme illustre dont l'œuvre vingt fois traduite est aussi douce à l'univers que le miel et que la paix! Son chapeau est trop large pour son front et lui rabat les oreilles." [13] When Proust read this chapter, he immediately assumed that Anatole France was the model and wrote to the author: "Tout le chapitre sur France (?) est extraordinaire." [14] His guess was probably accurate since Mme de Noailles, in publishing the letter, does not protest in a note, and the description in her book fits neatly even to topical points such as an allusion to France's activities in the Dreyfus Affair: "Son peuple l'a aimé; on l'a choisi et honoré dans d'importantes querelles." To approve so heartily of a disrespectful portrait of the great man suggests that the familiarity that Proust enjoyed with France bred a certain contempt. We can gather as much from the passages of *Temps perdu* where Proust analyzes with such keenness the character of Bergotte and the impression he makes in conversation. Léon Pierre-Quint tells us that Proust entertained his friends not only by reciting from memory whole pages of France but by telling anecdotes which he admitted would make a very amusing book.[15]

Proust basked in the warmth of so much reflected glory. Proud to be

insistence that the personality of a writer be judged apart from his social self, which Proust finds irrelevant if not inferior. This is the basis for his attack on Sainte-Beuve's method.

[13] Chap. II.

[14] *Correspondance générale*, II, 126.

[15] Pierre-Quint, p. 121.

able to number among his friends Anatole France and Robert de Montesquiou, he spared himself no pains to be obliging to both. Montesquiou used him in his efforts to gain a more intimate footing with France and his companions, to whose company Proust was freely admitted. The letters to Montesquiou record Proust's trotting back and forth, carrying messages with eager fidelity, and arranging meetings. His pains were in vain, however, for his aristocratic friend never succeeded in luring France to the Pavillon des Muses. Proust flattered his writer friends by drawing delicate analogies between their works. To oblige the Comtesse de Noailles, for example, he pointed out how much her character the Marquise d'Arpajon resembles the Putois of France.[16] Nothing delighted Proust more than to serve, and be agreeable to, those rare creatures who combined the two sublime qualities of literary and social distinction.

Through Mme de Caillavet's intercession—and cooperation in the writing—France consented to do a preface for *Les Plaisirs et les jours,* a work in which the author of *Thaïs* should have been able to recognize some of his own preciosity. However, Proust apparently had made little impression upon France, who accepted his homage in an absent-minded manner, and made no effort to seek his company or to understand him. Proust nevertheless greeted enthusiastically every new book that the master brought out, writing the bizarre letters of praise and self-abasement he was wont to inflict upon his acquaintances. A letter written sometime after the publication of *L'Anneau d'améthyste* is typical of Proust's inexhaustible eulogies. He declares France's latest book to be the greatest yet to come from his pen, proof that his genius is still growing. He calls France's work "la plus juste comédie humaine, la plus complète encyclopédie des mœurs du temps, les mémoires d'un Saint-Simon équitable et harmonieux. Aurait-on pu jamais prévoir que le don le plus rare de poésie qui fut jamais pût être un jour populaire? Cette gloire vous la connaissez. . . . Des mémoires vulgaires ont retenu les propos de M. Bergeret 'qui aime les cérémonies du culte.' Votre gaieté est goûtée des simples comme celle de Molière et de Cervantès. Et les raffinés n'y perdront rien." [17]

When his own book, *Swann,* appeared, Proust had not seen France for many years. He sent him, however, a copy with this dedication: "Au premier maître, au plus grand, au plus aimé." Impervious to such incense, France found the book unreadable and pretended hardly to remember the young man whom he had seen and talked to so often, and in whose home he had dined: "Je l'ai connu et j'ai préfacé, je crois, une de ses premières œuvres. C'est le fils d'un médecin hygiéniste au ministère de

[16] *Correspondance générale,* II, 97.

[17] See Jeanne-Marie Pouquet, *Le Salon de Mme Arman de Caillavet* (Hachette, 1926), p. 194.

l'Intérieur. Malheureusement, il paraît qu'il est devenu neurasthénique au dernier degré: il ne quitte pas son lit. Ses volets sont clos toute la journée et l'électricité toujours allumée. Je ne comprends rien à son œuvre. Il était agréable et plein d'esprit. Il avait un sens aigu de l'observation. Mais j'ai cessé de le fréquenter très vite." [18] France was far from suspecting that the book would one day be the most valuable in his entire library of 8000 titles. In 1939, when 250 of the choicest items were offered for sale, the Proust volume brought 24,000 francs.[19]

The ingratitude of the master never altered Proust's loyalty and devotion, for the roots of his esteem for France were too deep and too various. The Dreyfus case had offered further opportunity to increase France's prestige in Proust's eyes. Proust, a militant Dreyfusist, had solicited France's support in the struggle. At the time of the Goncourt award, when certain newspapers were attacking Proust as a conservative, he wrote to Paul Souday: "Je crois bien avoir été le premier dreyfusard, puisque c'est moi qui suis allé demander sa signature à Anatole France." [20] He never admired France more than in the role of defender of the persecuted. In the adulatory letter that Proust addressed to him for the political stand he was taking, the rhetoric cannot disguise the sincere feeling prompting Proust's effusions: ". . . vous ne pouvez plus envier au tragique grec d'avoir connu des victoires autres que les victoires littéraires." He contrasted France's disinterest with Chateaubriand's and Barrès's personal ambition: "Et, en effet, vous vous êtes mêlé à la vie publique d'une manière inconnue à ce siècle, ni comme Chateaubriand, ni comme Barrès, non pas pour vous faire un nom . . . [an action like the prose of *Thaïs*] parce que c'est aussi noble, parfaitement harmonieux et beau." [21]

While Proust was first drawn to France through his writings, it is clear that subsequently he found other reasons to admire him. One is curious to know how long he might have continued to write the name of Anatole France in the blank after the question, "Who is your favorite prose writer?" What was Proust's mature judgment of France as a writer? He suggests that he soon outgrew Bergotte's philosophy. Are we to infer that he continued to cultivate France merely because he enjoyed hobnobbing with a distinguished "vedette des dîners?" Although, for want of specific statement, we can only speculate, such a conclusion seems excessive. There is much in Anatole France that would always appeal to Proust, qualities he must have admired and affinities of thought and sensitivity that would insure his permanent sympathy.

[18] Quoted by Marcel LeGoff, *Anatole France à La Béchellerie* (Albin Michel, 1947), pp. 331-32.

[19] Suffel, p. 229.

[20] *Correspondance générale* (Plon, 1932), III, 71.

[21] Unpublished letter in the collection of M. Alfred Dupont. See Maurois, p. 96.

One doubts if the charm of *Le Livre de mon ami* could ever have completely failed to operate upon Proust. In that picture of a sensitive child, carefully brought up in an extremely bourgeois family, Proust must have seen his own childhood. Certain episodes such as the little boy's making a scene at bedtime, the death of the grandmother, sketchy and restrained in France, become enormous dramatic themes in *À La Recherche du temps perdu.* Proust made use of *Le Livre de mon ami* for his notes on Ruskin and in 1904 he wrote to Lauris to borrow a copy to read again.[22] The genteel, patrician attitudes of France created an atmosphere in which Proust would feel perfectly at home. The author of *Les Plaisirs et les jours* was temperamentally qualified to appreciate France's exquisite dilettantism. Proust's taste, cultivated by wide and discriminating reading, made him keenly sensitive to the beauties of France's style. Its classic restraint, its measure recall Racine, for whom both professed admiration and indebtedness. Both Proust and France loved words, the "paroles limpides" of Racine, words for themselves, beautiful and sonorous, charged with multiple meanings. The elegant Francian style represents the culmination of a long French tradition. In *Le Jardin d'Épicure* he describes it himself: "Le style simple est semblable à la clarté blanche. Il est complexe mais il n'y paraît pas." [23] By dint of infinite labor the verbal craftsman achieves a simplicity, a nudity of style, which translates exactly the clear idea. He "fait péniblement de la prose aisée." [24] One may say of France what Sainte-Beuve said of Racine: "le plus parfait modèle de ce style savant, châtié, poli, travaillé, dans l'enfantement duquel on arrive de la pensée à l'expression, lentement, par degrés, à force de tâtonnements et de ratures." [25]

Pierre Abraham has indicated features of Proust's style that seem inspired by France:

> Même souci de finir un paragraphe en beauté avec, ça et là, une pointe de préciosité qui, comme chez France, fait songer au concetto. Même souci de mêler dans les épithètes le sévère et le narquois. Témoin, dans la salle à manger de Balbec, ces invectives qui "réunissaient contre nous les touristes méprisants, dépeignés et furieux." Témoin la jeune laitière en chandail rouge dont le geste lui plaît "par sa rapidité familière, son apparence moelleuse et sa couleur écarlate." On se rapelle ce passage où, sous la plume de M. J.-J. Brousson, Antole France s'exprime ainsi: "Je prends le verbe le plus simple, le plus enfantin, celui qui indique le mieux le mouvement. Mais je soigne mes adjectifs. A quoi bon les multiplier pour dire la même chose? Si vous les prodiguez, contrariez-les. Vous surprendrez ainsi votre lecteur. N'écrivez pas: Des prélats magnifiques et pieux allèrent en procession. Mais: Des prélats obèses et pieux allèrent en procession. . . ." [26]

[22] Proust, *À Un Ami* (Amiot-Dumont, 1948), p. 53.
[23] France, *Oeuvres complètes* (Calmann-Lévy, 1948), IX, 443.
[24] Gabriel Des Hons, *Anatole France et Racine* (Colin, 1927), p. 265.
[25] *Ibid.*, p. 265. [26] Abraham, pp. 49-50.

The prose of Anatole France exemplifies the ideal of the generation of writers that constituted the masters of Proust's youth. France, Gourmont, Barrès, Bourget, Lemaître were writers of intelligence, observation, clarity and order, using a language of analysis and communication. The author of *A La Recherche du temps perdu* shared their curiosity concerning the human species, and utilized the language they had perfected to record the data of his observation. But before Proust died, a new esthetic, heralded by Symbolism and illustrated by Claudel, Gide, Valéry, and younger masters such as Jean Giraudoux, was rapidly gaining ground. Anatole France seemed to represent only the ultimate achievement of a defunct and surpassed esthetic.[27] The postwar generation was unsympathetic to France's cynicism and hostile to the stylistic ideal he represented. At best he was treated only as a "maître vénéré." In 1924 Gonzague Truc wrote a whole chapter on the "ingratitude contemporaine" toward Anatole France, pointing out that he had nothing to say to a generation putting action above intelligence and indifferent to perfections of style. Surrealists led the attack against the patriarch of letters. Their attitude is expressed by Philippe Soupault: "Ce scepticisme à l'eau de rose, cette perfection de style à bon marché représente pour moi tout ce qu'il y a de plus mauvais dans la littérature." [28] The Surrealist attitude represents, of course, the extreme of the reaction, and the general homage paid to France at the time of his death was far from perfunctory. Marcel Proust, who had been dead two years, would doubtless have been scandalized by words such as Soupault's, for although favorably disposed toward the new art, he was frequently made uneasy by its implications.

Proust's own position is between the old and the new. In sympathy with the esthetic ambitions of Symbolism and post-Symbolism, he endorsed in principle the poetic revolution. He was convinced that art, just as science, is progressive, and new artists must come to supplant the old. Yet he was too deeply rooted in the past to view without distress traditional values held for naught. The work he created is in itself a monument of transition, a product at once of the nineteenth-century novelistic tradition and of the esthetic that supplants it. Without being indifferent to the literary ideals that Anatole France represented, he realized that France represented the end of an epoch, and he incorporated in his own art principles and techniques that France could not comprehend.

[27] Note the judgment of Bouvard and Pécuchet, whom Proust borrows from Flaubert to echo the commonplaces of the enlightened public: "Quant à France, il écrit bien, mais pense mal, au contraire de Bourget, qui est profond, mais possède une forme affligeante." *Les Plaisirs et les jours* (Gallimard, 1924), p. 102.

[28] Pierre Varillon and Henri Rambaud, *Enquête sur les maîtres de la jeune littérature* (Bloud et Gay, 1923), p. 195.

Robert de Montesquiou

Robert, Comte de Montesquiou-Fesenzac, was born in Paris, March 18, 1855, and died September 11, 1921, at Menton. During forty of his sixty-six years, Montesquiou occupied one of the most prominent positions in Parisian society. For *fin de siècle* elegance and snobbery he had no equal. He lived only for the exquisite: in its name he meted out chastisement to the awkward and the vulgar. Yet his own taste was not always of the surest, and persons who did not fear him generally found him ridiculous. He squandered a fortune and his whole life in a vain attempt to make society concur in his opinion of himself. "Mal compris, mal aimé, mal connu, mécontent," thus Montesquiou described himself.[29] He died embittered by the incomprehension of his contemporaries. Posterity was to deal far worse with him. The immortality he sought on the grounds of a sizable literary production not devoid of merit, he obtained only by being identified as the model for the grotesque Charlus of Proust's novel.[30]

The name of Montesquiou-Fesenzac is a very proud one. Under Louis XV the family established its descent from Clovis. There have been many members of particular distinction, such as Blaise de Montluc; Pierre de Montesquiou, the conqueror of Savoy; the Chevalier d'Artagnan, hero of *Les Trois Mousquetaires*; the father of Théophile Gautier; the governess of the King of Rome.[31] Robert, the heir to so many glories, took his position very seriously. With money adequate to sustain his pretensions, he established himself as a twentieth-century *grand seigneur.* Elisabeth de Gramont describes her early encounter with Montesquiou at St. Moritz. The young girl noticed the haughty expression of his bold features and his little black teeth; she was particularly impressed by the recherché elegance of his costume and his single ring.[32] One remembers how taken Proust would be with Montesquiou's boutonnieres, especially the moss rose.[33] His sartorial inclination favored the eccentric. People had so come to expect his greens and pinks that once when he arrived to give a lecture, dressed in sober black, something like general dismay crept over the audience. Montesquiou was charmed with the effect he had produced.

[29] Louis Thomas, *L'Esprit de Montesquiou* (Mercure de France, 1943), Preface.

[30] "Personalité des plus curieuses, parce qu'entièrement factice, d'une époque de travestis éclatants et de mensonges pieux ou impies, il ne demeura que grâce au *Des Esseintes* de Huysmans et au *Baron de Charlus* de Proust." Paul Morand, "*1900*" (Editions de France, 1931), p. 232.

[31] Thomas, Preface.

[32] Duchesse de Clermont-Tonnerre, *Robert de Montesquiou et Marcel Proust* (Flammarion, 1925), Chap. II.

[33] *Correspondance générale* (Plon, 1930), I, 225. (Cf. *À L'Ombre des jeunes filles en fleurs,* II, 188: first portrait of Charlus.)

He explained to Proust afterward: "Je tenais à éveiller ce sentiment: l'attente du ridicule déçue." Proust found the count astounding and wrote his friend Robert Dreyfus: "M. de Montesquiou . . . fait œuvre d'art avec son ridicule et l'a merveilleusement stylisé." [34]

The attention Montesquiou lavished on his person was not greater than his expenditures on his dwelling, the Pavillon des Muses, which was in Neuilly on the boulevard that now bears the name of Montesquiou's neighbor, Maurice Barrès. During Montesquiou's occupancy it was famous for its mirrors, its enormous hydrangeas, the fabulous collections of glass, books, and porcelains that it contained. Privileged visitors remember a sleigh in the drawing room, and a great Chinese dragon bed, with claws holding the mattress and eyes that lighted up most fiercely. Montesquiou lived there with Yturri, his secretary and companion for twenty years. Yturri was an exotically handsome person, originally from South America, but was a clerk in a Paris department store when Montesquiou first met him. His taste was better than his protector's, and as long as he lived, the decorations at the Pavillon des Muses benefited from his restraining influence. When he died of tuberculosis, Montesquiou erected a sumptuous monument in the Petit-Montreuil cemetery of Versailles. In Yturri he had lost a faithful companion and servitor. He could look back upon the years with him as his most brilliant period. Yturri had bargained for the *objets d'art* Montesquiou acquired and managed the household; he had taken care of much of the correspondence and arranged the receptions, dinners, parties which assembled at no. 98 boulevard Maillot the *haut monde* of Paris.[35]

Montesquiou was always the lion of the party whether he was host or guest. His conversation was scintillating but, as frequently the case, something of a trial for others. Moreover, no one knew when he might be the butt of one of Montesquiou's cruel jokes. In France, where cattiness, if one of the minor vices, is also one of the major social arts, the tongue of Robert de Montesquiou was considered a rapier. His insolence was all the more effective since it was expressed so elegantly. Pierre Veber wrote that "M. de Montesquiou est le maître de la perfidie courtoise: il excelle à lancer des méchancetés polies et un peu lyriques. Ce poète excelle à trouver des images rares, même quand il veut être désagréable à quelqu'un." [36] Frequently his devastating remarks took the form of aphorisms. There are Wildean mots ascribed to him such as: the trouble with *arrivistes* is not that they arrive, but that they never leave. He avenged himself for the success of other writers by carving little netsukes of venom

[34] *Correspondance générale* (Plon, 1933), IV, 212.
[35] See Pierre-Quint, pp. 67 ff.
[36] Thomas, Preface. The source for the following anecdotes is likewise Thomas.

such as: "De certains fonds de Zola donnent à penser: si le sale perd sa force, avec quoi salira-t-on?" "La maison de Molière est devenue les Ecuries d'Augier." Most to be feared were his very personal attacks on members of society which took the form of macaronic verse:

Ne laissez pas sans lumières
Vos fils à Robert d'Humières.
. . . .

Le jeune Lucien Daudet
Autour des princes rôdait.

He called these malicious gems "papillotes mondaines" and recorded them carefully on cards.

Typical of the scandal this jovial gentleman was fond of creating is the lecture he gave at the showing of the *Film immobile,* a series of painted wooden silhouettes representing "Tout-Paris au Bois." Almost all the personalities involved were present in the audience. Montesquiou's acid comments were so many arrows shot about the hall and created consternation and indignation on all sides. The Faubourg Saint-Germain never forgave Montesquiou for being its terrible gadfly. He had made particular fun of the new Jewish elements, and the Jews, in revenge, helped to blackball him and mire his literary reputation through newspapers and journals like the *Revue de Paris.* Society made him pay dearly for his pranks and his insults.

In frustrating Montesquiou's literary ambition, his victims struck at his most vulnerable part. For, in his elegant way, he served the Muse faithfully. Proust told Montesquiou once that he was more than the exquisite decadent he was supposed to be—had energy and a creative force, a seventeenth-century habit of thinking in verse.[37] In spite of Proust's kind words, and their occasional survival in some anthology, no one now reads Montesquiou's precious verses. They are interesting, nevertheless, not so much for intrinsic value (although they are not quite without merit) as for their evocation of *fin de siècle* opulence and extravagance. Of his many de luxe, privately printed collections the best known are perhaps the *Chauves-souris,* the *Hortensias bleus,* the *Chef des odeurs suaves, Parcours du rêve au souvenir.* Montesquiou was fond of reading his verse before the most select gatherings of intelligentsia and *cognoscenti,* and spared no pains to collect just the right people. He could, moreover, as we have observed, be persuaded to give public lectures on Oriental art and many other subjects of refined, cultural interest. It would be amusing to know more of his lecture tour in America. He presented himself before the culture-hungry matrons of Boston, New York, and

[37] *Correspondance générale,* I, 4.

Philadelphia, spending in all about a month in this "grande barbarie éclairée de gaz" of ours.

The success, the *gloire*, that so many ancestors, so many talents, should by rights win him, refused to come to rest upon Montesquiou's proud shoulders. He coveted the Academy, but would not make a gesture in its direction. When Heredia died in 1905, Montesquiou waited for the delegation to come for him at his country seat, Artagnan, in the Hautes Pyrénées, but he waited in vain. This unhappy man was doomed never to be esteemed and appreciated as he thought he deserved. He graciously mingled with the *gratin* of the social and artistic worlds, knowing that his presence lent distinction to any gathering. Sarah Bernhardt, Diaghileff, Ida Rubenstein, and D'Annunzio were among his close acquaintances. Isadora Duncan asked him to give her a child to cure her neurasthenia. But people he really esteemed snubbed him. Anatole France, in spite of Proust's pleadings, wanted nothing to do with the count. Time and again he refused Montesquiou's invitations, and once at a luncheon when he saw Montesquiou enter the room, he left muttering, "Je ne peux pas supporter cet homme qui me parle toujours de ses ancêtres." [38] Montesquiou could not count on many persons like Barrès, who always treated him with deference. The Palais Rose, to which he moved after leaving the Pavillon des Muses, was never so brilliant as its predecessor. At the last grand soiree given in the new residence no guest appeared, for someone of malicious intent had sent word to the papers that the party had been called off. Montesquiou never entertained again.

Proust met Montesquiou at Madeleine Lemaire's in 1893. Montesquiou had just published the *Chauves-souris* and *Chef des odeurs suaves*. His intelligence and his artistic judgment captivated Proust. Moreover, climber that Proust was, he was greatly impressed by Montesquiou's social position. As *arbiter elegantiarum*, Montesquiou could open all doors for him, introduce him to such goddesses of high society as the Comtesse Greffulhe and the Princesse de Wagram, prototypes of the Duchesse de Guermantes.

Proust's letters to Montesquiou are remarkable examples of toadyism and pedantry. Enchanted at being an intimate of such an elegant gentleman, Proust garnished his letters with literary references to impress his correspondent and to honor him by recklessly placing in the scales opposite Montesquiou's work, the masterpieces of literature. It is scandalous to observe Proust's readiness to dash to pieces the statues of great writers in order to place any of his friends' likenesses in their stead:

"Corneille a-t-il fait un plus beau vers que celui-ci. . . ." [39]

[38] Clermont-Tonnerre, p. 213.
[39] *Correspondance générale*, I, 4.

"Ces vers admirables dont quelques-uns ont la fervente pureté des plus beaux vers de Villon. . . ."[40]

"Je crois . . . que pour Baudelaire et pour vous."[41]

He began his campaign to win over the count by begging his leave to write a eulogistic article bearing the startling title "De La Simplicité de M. de Montesquiou." He expressed his earnest desire to be allowed to call in person, to obtain Montesquiou's advice regarding the article "de vive voix."[42] In spite of all his pains, Proust was unable to place his article. He carried it back and forth between the *Revue Blanche* and the *Revue de Paris* for weeks without arousing any interest. Many years later he wrote another article, and this time he was more successful. In 1905 the magazine *Arts de la Vie* carried his study on Montesquiou, entitled "Un Professeur de Beauté."

As antidote for his obsequiousness toward Montesquiou, Proust had recourse to his engaging accomplishment of mimicry. Behind the count's back, Proust obliged his friends with imitations. Of course wind of his impudence got back to his victim's aristocratic nostrils, and Proust was sharply reprimanded. The only time Proust really stood up to the count was in connection with the Dreyfus case. He would not condone any disparagement of the Jews. In polite but forthright language he stated his position: "Je n'ai pas répondu hier à ce que vous m'avez demandé des juifs. C'est pour cette raison très simple: si je suis catholique comme mon père et mon frère, par contre, ma mère est juive."[43] Elsewhere his expressions of righteous indignation are limited to little digs and sullen retorts. Letter LXXXII to Montesquiou is an excellent example. Montesquiou had made fun of Proust's interminable scrawls by referring to Solomon watching the ants file by. Proust, stung by the comparison, wrote that it was just like the count to assume the "beau rôle," and leave for others that of vile insects! But he closed his message with his customary courtesy, signing "Votre admirateur affectueux. . . ."[44] Even after Proust had gained prestige and self-assurance and had no longer any need of the irascible count, he continued to accept his scoldings with infinite patience. Proust was basically a coward and the devious way was most natural to him.

The years had brought about a reversal of their roles, however. If, at least for a time during his youth, Proust would have given anything to

[40] *Ibid.*, p. 23.
[41] *Ibid.*, p. 4.
[42] *Ibid.*, p. 45.
[43] *Ibid.*, pp. 100-101.
[44] *Ibid.*, pp. 74-75. Montesquiou recounted the episode in his memoirs, *Les Pas effacés* (Emile Paul, 1923), II, 284-85.

occupy the position in society and the arts that was Montesquiou's, now Montesquiou coveted Proust's literary success. It is now Proust who is sought after. During the war years he complained to his other friends about the count's too numerous letters. They had not seen each other for a long time. Proust had never gone to the Palais Rose, nor did he encourage Montesquiou to call upon him. Once, during the first year of the war, after much solicitation, Proust received Montesquiou. The visit, supposed to last five minutes, stretched into seven hours. They never met again, but there were letters right up to the end.

Proust's mounting fame made the realization of his own lack of success almost unendurably painful to the unhappy count. At times he tried to make jokes: "Je voudrais bien un peu de gloire, moi aussi. Je ne devrais plus m'appeler que Montesproust." [45] But usually he could not control the floods of bitterness and spite that praise of Proust would release. He sneered at Proust's bourgeois origins, his Jewish blood, his snobbery, his handwriting, and his dress. He let it be known he thought the publicity for *Swann* was a scandal, that its success was due to personal friends, a bought press. With hiccups of rage he lashed out at the work itself: "un livre touffu, inextricable . . . où il y a de jolies choses, entrecoupées d'horreurs, comme à plaisir, plaisir un peu sadique, puisque les premières sont des souvenirs de famille, et, les secondes, des scènes de saphisme, le tout finissant par tourner au pandémonium, faute de rédaction, de goût et de choix." Its author will never give his "measure," for "sa mesure consiste peut-être précisément à n'en pas avoir." [46] Moreover, he is always sick, "au moins toujours au lit, entouré d'appareils respiratoires pour conjurer des crises d'asthme; il y a aussi des pots de confiture et des pots de chambre." [47]

Proust was too ill, or too conscious of his glory, to react to the count's abuse. Only when he suspected Montesquiou might be going to slander him in his autobiography did he indicate any concern. He wrote to Paul Brach in effect: "Pensez-vous que si Montesquiou m'attaque dans ses *Mémoires*, je puisse faire un procès . . . ?" [48] Proust must have felt quits with Montesquiou once and for all after he had drawn his portrait as the Baron Charlus. Montesquiou recognized himself at once. Henri Bardac tells how Montesquiou asked him suspiciously: "Quel est cet étonnant bonhomme, ce merveilleux fantoche qui fait son apparition sur la plage de Balbec?" [49] Bardac lost no time in reporting the incident

[45] Clermont-Tonnerre, p. 216.
[46] *Les Pas effacés*, II, 284.
[47] *Ibid.*, p. 286.
[48] Proust, "Lettres inédites," *Revue Universelle*, April 1, 1928, p. 13.
[49] Bardac, "Proust et Montesquiou," *Revue de Paris*, September, 1948, p. 145.

to Proust, who laughed, and, clasping his hands beneath his chin, recited with mock gravity the lines of La Fontaine:

> Craignez, Romains, craignez que le Ciel quelque jour
> Ne transporte chez vous les pleurs et la misère
> Et mettant en nos mains par un juste retour
> Les armes dont se sert sa vengeance sévère.[50]

Proust had his revenge for the years of humiliation he had suffered at the hands of the count; and, although he was not above enjoying it fully, apparently bore him no grudge. Upon several occasions he warmly recommended Montesquiou's talents and tried to do him favors. He declared him to be the best art critic of the times. To Jacques Boulenger he wrote on his behalf: "On épaissit autour de sa vieillesse (démunie, de plus, d'argent, je crois) le plus injuste des silences, car c'est un critique d'art, un essayiste merveilleux, qui peint comme personne, en prose, l'œuvre d'un peintre, d'un sculpteur qu'il aime." [51] Boulenger, obligingly, although unenthusiastically, consented to accept something by Montesquiou for the *Revue de la Semaine*. But Proust's kind intentions miscarried. For some reason unknown to Proust, Montesquiou greeted the overtures with a fit of rage that put an end to the negotiations.

In Proust's letters to Boulenger, written the year before Proust died, we have a curious glimpse of his feelings toward the count. He explained to Boulenger that he had met Montesquiou when he was so young that he always had retained for him the respect one owes to a "grande personne." The contrast between Montesquiou's obscurity and his own fame made him highly uncomfortable. "Navré de cette espèce d'ostracisme dont il est victime, chaque fois qu'on parle de moi dans un journal, je me dis: 'Comme cela doit le fâcher.'" [52]

Before death overtook them, Proust earnestly desired to make his peace with Montesquiou. He thanked Montesquiou for the flowers he had sent to him, the invalid "qui n'est pas aigri," [53] and expressed his earnest wish to hear that Montesquiou himself was feeling better. He then went back over the past, trying to assuage the count, who was still bitter over Proust's imitations, his "singeries." Finally, like the droll little mannikin he had been in 1893, the dying Proust begged leave to make his last bow before the count: "Et mourant de fatigue, permettez-moi, après tant de saluts et inclinaisons, de vous tirer, très respectueusement, une dernière révérence. Votre admirateur et ami, Marcel Proust." [54]

[50] *Ibid.*, p. 146.
[51] *Correspondance générale*, III, 253.
[52] *Ibid.*, p. 254.
[53] *Ibid.*, I, 283.
[54] *Ibid.*, p. 287.

For almost thirty years Proust and Montesquiou had known each other. The benefits were almost all one-sided. Montesquiou, with a fatuousness and obtuseness scarcely credible, could recognize in Proust only a disciple whose talents were best employed in singing the praises of Montesquiou's own exalted person. He recalled in his memoirs the pretty description of one of his parties that his guest Proust had written. And he added: "Il a écrit la plus caractéristique de toutes les phrases qui m'aient été consacrées par des contemporains. La voici: 'Vous vous élevez au-dessus de l'inimitié, comme le goéland au-dessus de la tempête, et vous souffririez d'être privé de cette pression ascendante.' Si l'homme qui a écrit ces lignes avait été, tout le temps, cet homme-là, et rédigé un livre tout de cette pénétration, comme de ce style, ce livre aurait été un chef-d'œuvre." [55] Montesquiou probably did not know just how much Proust really owed to him. Could he recognize in Proust his own way of playing with ideas and suggesting all sorts of nuances? Did he know the guide that he had been to Proust in art appreciation and criticism? Montesquiou was not only a model for Proust but a real master, a "professeur de Beauté" as Proust had called him. But the pupil was a genius and soon surpassed the master, who was, after all, only an esthete. Montesquiou was left behind to ruminate the folly of putting more talent into his life than into his works.

Anna de Noailles

Proust's long acquaintance with Mme de Noailles dates from the last years of the century. In 1893, during one of his rare travels, he had met the Princesse de Brancovan, but it was probably several years later before he encountered in society her daughters who were to become the Comtesse de Noailles and the Princesse de Caraman-Chimay.

Proust delighted in the company of these two charming and highborn young ladies, paying court particularly to Anna, whose poetry and beauty were creating for her an increasing number of enthusiastic admirers.[56] Proust's gallantry and regard for her social position made his compliments to her talents the most lavish to flow from his habitually generous pen. But his praise, although ludicrously excessive, was probably sincere, for the ardor that is evident in his letters to Noailles did not cool even when he spoke of her to others. Moreover, excessive admiration for other people is fundamental in his morbidly self-deprecatory personality. Very early in life he developed the habit of attributing to his friends sublime virtues and ostentatiously humbling himself before them. The victims of

[55] *Les Pas effacés*, II, 285-86.

[56] The portrait of the Vicomtesse Gaspard de Réveillon in *Jean Santeuil*, II, 304-13, must be that of Mme de Noailles as a bride.

his suffocating caresses often felt irritated and embarrassed, or at least feigned so. Robert Dreyfus makes the most eloquent statement of the Proustian hyperbole which vitiated his judgments of his friends' works:

> Ces éloges accablants, multipliés, terribles,—comparables à ceux que le Titan Hugo fit subir à tant de *poetae minores,* coupables seulement de lui avoir soumis leurs vers,—n'abusèrent jamais personne (ou presque personne). Tous les amis de Marcel Proust les ont éprouvés comme moi, sans y attacher d'importance. C'était sa manière: on le savait sincère, mais exagérateur. Il y avait en lui tant de puissance du cœur qu'en appelant un instant à son niveau les élus de son amitié ou de son imagination, il les élevait aux nues comme par jeu; mais il leur laissait le soin de rester à jamais dupes de sa générosité, ou de savoir redescendre à terre. Souvent aussi, par bonheur, son ardent besoin de dire la vérité l'emportait encore sur son désir de plaire; il devenait, à lui seul Alceste et Philinte. Alors il mêlait à l'éloge une rapide moquerie aiguë et dense, enveloppée pourtant de précautions si indulgentes qu'on ne lui était pas moins obligé de remettre les choses au point par ses doux sarcasmes que de vous étourdir par ses compliments.[57]

Throughout the collection of his letters that she published, Mme de Noailles makes little protesting and chiding exclamations, for nowhere did Proust burn stronger incense than before her.

In spite of his flattery, perhaps because of it, Proust's judgment was eagerly sought by the proud and gifted spirits in whose company he ingratiated himself. Not only was he the *arbiter elegantiarum* after Montesquiou, but his word was heeded in all literary and artistic matters. Mme de Noailles, in her *Portrait de Marcel Proust,* testifies to the remarkable authority with which he was invested. She pays full tribute to Proust's inspiring influence: "Sans Marcel Proust . . . je n'eusse pas écrit les poèmes que la prédilection de Marcel Proust réclamait. Son éblouissante amitié m'a influencée, modifiée, comme seul en est capable un noble amour du verbe." [58]

Do the letters reveal this critical faculty or this inspiration to which Mme de Noailles appears so sensitive? Let us see. They contain discussion of her principal works. Letters of 1901 refer to the *Cœur innombrable*; of 1902, *Ombre des jours*; of 1904, *Visage émerveillé*; of 1905, *Domination*; of 1907, *Eblouissements.* An occasional remark is all we can detect of adverse criticism. And then it is in the form of a compliment, since it refers to a fault overcome. In 1906 Proust congratulated her on some verse, remarking that it was superior to some she had written earlier in which he had perceived "quelque chose d'un peu subjectif dans l'inspiration et parfois trop discontinu dans l'expression malgré presque tout admirable." This tender barb merits a comment from the countess, who

[57] Dreyfus, *Souvenirs sur Marcel Proust* (Grasset, 1926), pp. 145-46.

[58] *Correspondance générale,* II, 7.

calls attention to Proust's "infaillible sens critique." One must agree regretfully with her that "les forces de l'amitié . . . refoulent et baîllonnent son libre jugement."[59] There is little in Proust's letters except raving praise, delirious hymns of adoration, which, were it not merely the jargon of the *précieux*, would incline one to think that the overpowering beauty of Noailles's poetry brought Proust dangerously close to fits and foaming. In his frenzy, he sees France's greatest nature poets as only unworthy ancestors of the new poetess: "Sur deux cents vers de Lamartine, on en trouve deux donnant une impression exacte de nature. Vous, *chaque vers*."[60] In *Atala* there are two or three perfectly beautiful images. "Il y en a dans chacune de vos pages autant que de façons de dire."[61] Nothing in the letters proves that Noailles submitted manuscripts to Proust or discussed her works with him before she presented him with a dedicated copy. Despite her testimony to Proust's critical acumen, it does not appear that she made full use of it.

If we cannot find in Proust anything like a fair estimate of Mme de Noailles's poetry, we can discover something about his interests and standards, which are, after all, of more importance to us. The works that prompt his observations are of only incidental interest, reminding us for a moment of a literary creation that a short while ago was full of life, but that has not lived so long as the praise it evoked. What does Proust find so remarkable about Noailles's writing? Its beauty. The word recurs on every page. Although it is scarcely remarkable to find beauty mentioned in connection with literary judgments, Proust uses the word so frequently and so exclusively that it requires particular elucidation. It would be incorrect to assume that Proust was a pure esthete. He protested against such an interpretation of Ruskin's cult of beauty: we may do the same for him. Proust separates Ruskin sharply from all dilettantes and esthetes who devote themselves exclusively to the pleasure of works of art. Beauty should not be loved merely for the pleasure it gives. For Ruskin—and for Proust—it held the supreme and eternal reality: "Mais cette Beauté à laquelle il se trouva ainsi consacrer sa vie ne fut pas conçue par lui comme un objet de jouissance fait pour la charmer, mais comme une réalité infiniment plus importante que la vie, pour laquelle il aurait donné la sienne."[62] Proust's notion of beauty implies the metaphysical. It is given to the artist to perceive eternal reality intuitively through inspiration. His talent serves to fix the inner vision in a communicable form. Thus Proust's repeated use of the word "beautiful" is more

[59] *Ibid.*, p. 144.
[60] *Ibid.*, p. 162.
[61] *Ibid.*, pp. 76-77.
[62] *Pastiches et mélanges*, p. 155.

significant than it first appears. It must be taken in the very loftiest sense. "Le plaisir esthétique est précisément celui qui accompagne la découverte d'une vérité." [63] The miracle of artistic creation is the glimpse that beauty affords of the eternal.

Proust paid homage to Noailles as a great artist who creates and cultivates the beautiful by use of language. He put her novels higher than her verse, but what he appreciated in them is their poetry or their verbal magic. In the *Nouvelle Espérance* "un génie novateur et violent a dissocié toutes les façons de dire, de composer, de penser, anciennes." [64] In her next volume, the *Visage émerveillé,* Proust beheld the reconstruction, the creation, of a new idiom. Each writer, he affirmed, must thus destroy the old. Language does not exist outside of writers, and they are authorized, even commanded, to alter it to their own purpose: "Chaque écrivain est obligé de se faire sa langue. . . . Ils ne commencent à écrire bien qu'à condition d'être originaux, de faire eux-mêmes leur langue. La correction, la perfection du style existe, mais au delà de l'originalité, après avoir traversé les faits, non en deçà." [65]

Noailles's sensitivity to color and nuance enchanted Proust. He called it her impressionism and praised the unity of tone she achieved. He declared of the *Visage émerveillé* "qu'il n'est pas composé de parties, qu'il est un, baigné dans une même atmosphère, baigné tout entier, où les couleurs se commandent les unes les autres. . . . Cette vérité géniale de la couleur fait de vous le plus grand des impressionistes." This multicolored unity may be taken as the material symbol of a mysterious primordial harmony which is the mark of masterpieces. Proust's elaboration on this idea merits quotation in full:

> Si on cherche ce qui fait la beauté absolue de certaines choses, des fables de La Fontaine, des comédies de Molière, on voit que ce n'est pas la profondeur, ou telle ou telle autre vertu qui semble éminente. Non, c'est une espèce de fondu, d'unité transparente, où toutes les choses, perdant leur premier aspect de choses, sont venues se ranger les unes à côté des autres dans une espèce d'ordre, pénétrées de la même lumière, vues les unes dans les autres, sans un seul mot qui reste en dehors, qui soit resté réfractaire à cette assimilation (je sens que je suis moi-même incompréhensible à force de mal dire, mais cette idée me vient pour la première fois et je ne sais comment l'exprimer). Je suppose que c'est ce qu'on appelle le Vernis des Maîtres, et c'est ce que possède à un degré inoui et avec une fraîcheur de couleur éblouissante le *Visage émerveillé!* [66]

The stamp of great works, which Proust thought he recognized in *Visage émerveillé,* consists of "une espèce de vision géniale qui crée d'une façon constante." [67] Style is vision, he was fond of declaring.

[63] *Ibid.,* p. 185. [64] *Correspondance générale,* II, 75.
[65] *Ibid.* (Plon, 1936), VI, 93. [66] *Ibid.,* II, 86-87. [67] *Ibid.,* p. 76.

Rereading the Comtesse de Noailles's novel *Domination* is like leafing through an old plush-covered photograph album. How dated it has become! Half-smothered in *fin de siècle* ornamentation and fine writing, the story follows pantingly the amorous and professional career of a hothouse Julien Sorel. Antoine Arnault is a puny descendant of Stendhal's man of destiny and Chateaubriand's heroes, sick with the century. Cut away from Mme de Noailles's lush poetry, his adventures seem as unsavory as those recounted in *Les Liaisons dangereuses.* Yet this simpering novel, built largely from literary souvenirs, called forth from Proust the greatest eulogies, somewhat to the countess' embarrassment, for she was not unaware of the novel's limitations and refused a second edition. But it was Proust's favorite, and he never tired talking about it. "C'est peut-être la plus grande beauté littéraire que je connaisse." [68] Can Proust's enthusiasm be attributed entirely to his desire to please? I think not, for the qualities that make it unacceptable today would have delighted the author of *Les Plaisirs et les jours*: quintessential refinement and elegance coupled with viciousness and ennui depicted in voluptuous prose.

Proust hastened to write his first impressions to the author. The death scene caused him great anguish: "Calme depuis des années, quelles souffrances ce livre ne me rend-il pas et pour combien d'années! Je suis encore bien brisé de l'agonie d'Elisabeth pour vous écrire sur tout cela." [69] He moves away, accordingly, from this painful subject to more mundane matters. How could she dare, he asks, show great ladies who shared their lovers with their attendants, since society would be apt to draw parallels among her friends? Then he slyly comments on her placing of dinner guests in the novel. The sycophant, pleased to be on confidential terms with the nobility, asks how she will henceforth dare face "les roturiers qui dîneront chez vous et que vous placerez après Turenne." [70] Some vague and high-flown comments on her "sublime style," and Proust brings this epistle to a close that is as fatuous and groveling as the rest: "Au revoir, Madame. . . . Qu'il y a longtemps que j'aurais aimé vous revoir! . . . Mais détesté du mari charmant, qui a si juste et légitime influence, honni de Mme Bulteau, comment même m'envoyez-vous votre livre?" [71]

A succeeding letter is more serious and touches on some basic esthetic matters. Although disagreeing generally with the critic Rageot, who found the style of *Domination* to be indebted to Barrès, Proust does think that her use of the present where one might expect the perfect or imperfect resembles Barrès's. He has had to destroy some of his own writing because of its resemblance to Noailles's style, for unintentional pastiches are Proust's particular *bête noire*:

[68] *Ibid.*, p. 114. [69] *Ibid.*, p. 112.
[70] *Ibid.*, p. 115. [71] *Ibid.*, p. 117.

Or je suis l'ennemi de tout pastiche, excepté quand il est voulu, et encore! Enfin, et surtout, et je l'avais même écrit à Madame de Noailles, elle a, à mon avis, pour au moins une durée de cinquante ans, supprimé pour tout autre, la possibilité de s'adresser, en discours direct à des villes, etc. . . . Tout ce qu'on fera dans ce genre, sous cette forme, si sincère, vécu, antérieur à elle que cela soit, et à moins qu'en descendant longuement et profondément en soi-même au cœur de son cœur, ou plutôt au cerveau de son cœur, on ne trouve une expression différente et entièrement individuelle, tout aura l'air imité d'elle, son rayonnement boira toutes nos clartés. Je dis 'nos' bien prétentieusement, parce que moi-même, j'ai dû brûler presque un volume sur la Bretagne, écrit avant d'avoir jamais rien lu d'elle et où les

Quimperlé! . . .
Pont-Aven!

semblaient venir de l'*Ombre des Jours* ou de la *Domination*.[72]

Proust finds Noailles's picture of Bruges and of Venice vastly different from Barrès's, and states that for years to come their two visions will impose themselves upon all notions of the two cities.[73] "Ce miracle d'une vue de génie qui s'interpose" is one of the esthetic phenomena which most interest Proust. The poet affords one a glimpse of a "marvelous city, different from the rest of the world." "Le suprême effort de l'écrivain . . . n'aboutit qu'à soulever partiellement pour nous le voile de laideur et d'insignifiance qui nous laisse incurieux devant l'univers." So by a sort of clairvoyance the poet can see that which is veiled from us until he opens our eyes. Does he see things that others cannot? Is his garden actually more beautiful than our own? "'Menez-nous,' voudrions-nous pouvoir dire à M. Maeterlinck, à Mme de Noailles, 'dans le jardin de Zélande où croissent les fleurs démodées,' sur la route parfumée 'de trèfle et d'armoise.'" [74] No, the poet's garden is just any garden. The secret of its charm lies in the reflection of genius upon it:

Par l'art seulement, nous pouvons sortir de nous, savoir ce que voit un autre de cet univers qui n'est pas le même que le nôtre et dont les paysages nous seraient restés aussi inconnus que ceux qu'il peut y avoir dans la lune. Grâce à l'art, au lieu de voir un seul monde, le nôtre, nous le voyons se multiplier, et autant qu'il y a d'artistes originaux, autant nous avons de mondes à notre disposition, plus différents les uns des autres que ceux qui roulent dans l'infini, et qui bien des siècles après qu'est éteint le foyer dont ils émanaient, qu'il s'appelât Rembrandt ou Ver Meer, nous envoient leur rayon spécial.[75]

[72] Princesse Bibesco, *Au Bal avec Marcel Proust* (Gallimard, 1928), pp. 58-59. Is what Proust destroyed a part of *Jean Santeuil?* See Henri Bonnet, "A quel moment fut composé *Jean Santeuil*," *Bulletin de la Société des Amis de Marcel Proust*, III (1953), 80.

[73] Léon Blum compares her depiction of Venice to that of D'Annunzio's: "Venise enflammée comme celle de d'Annunzio." "L'Oeuvre poétique de la Comtesse de Noailles," *Revue de Paris*, January 15, 1908, p. 242. Blum's study can be recommended as an excellent appreciation of Noailles's place in modern poetry.

[74] *Pastiches et mélanges*, p. 249.

[75] *Le Temps retrouvé* (Gallimard, 1927), II, 43-44.

The essay on the *Eblouissements*, which appeared in *Figaro*, June, 1907, is characteristic of Proust's exquisite criticism.[76] He composes a choice bouquet for the ardent countess, the sort which is no longer in fashion among critics but which may still appeal to those not irritated by Proust's fine manners or to those willing to overlook them in hopes of finding refreshing and stimulating comments. The article is built on conceits, pleasantly and skillfully executed. In an epoch of beards, eye-glasses, derby hats, Proust observes, there is always a ludicrous incongruity between the poet and his poetry: "Dans notre triste époque, sous nos climats, les poètes, j'entends les poètes hommes, dans le même moment où ils jettent sur les champs en fleurs un regard extasié, sont obligés en quelque sorte de s'excepter de la beauté universelle, de s'exclure, par l'imagination, du paysage." The poet must exclude his ugly person and invent a character to recite his lovely verses. Mme de Noailles suffers under no such handicap.[77] "Elle n'est pas la moins délicieuse des mille beautés dont resplendit un radieux jardin d'été où elle se confond." She is at once the poet and the heroine: she can express herself without any fiction, with all the more effectiveness. She is Racine and his princess, Chénier and his young captive. Yet she scrupulously avoids too personal or too specific references, never revealing her social or contingent self, as it were: "De sorte qu'il n'y a pas de livre où le moi tienne autant de place, et aussi peu: ou en tienne autant, nous verrons comment tout à l'heure, le moi profond qui individualise les œuvres et les fait durer, si peu le moi qu'on a défini d'un seul mot en disant qu'il était haïssable."

The second part of Proust's essay, on the Six Gardens of Paradise, holds most interest. Of all nature poets', the countess' garden is the most natural. She approaches nature directly through sentiment. Nothing but poetry in her garden. In the others where Proust allows his eye to roam, a less pure, a less direct, inspiration prevails. John Ruskin's garden he cannot discuss here; Maeterlinck's, despite its great beauties, reveals extra-poetic ambitions and interests; Régnier's is filled with sculpture and architecture; Jammes's is a monument to botany and religion; Monet's a place of tones and colors rather than of flowers. The sustained conceit of the gardens is not only a pretty tribute to the Comtesse de Noailles but an accurate and suggestive characterization of the artists mentioned. Another page worth retaining of this essay is the discussion of metaphors. Proust first speaks of metaphors based upon mistaken perception, the most primitive and the least contrived of all imagery:

> Dans vos taillis serrés où la pie en sifflant
> Roule sous les sapins comme un fruit noir et blanc.

[76] *Correspondance générale*, II, 225-41.

[77] Nor did the chief of the Symbolists, Jean Moréas. He used to declare, "Lé poètte doit être bo, jé suis bo!" (André Billy, *L'Epoque 1900* [Tallandier, 1951], p. 334.)

" Métaphores [Proust says] qui recomposent et nous rendent le mensonge de notre première impression, quand, nous promenant dans un bois ou suivant les bords d'une rivière, nous avons pensé d'abord, en entendant rouler quelque chose, que c'était quelque fruit, et non un oiseau." Such comparisons, in substituting what we have felt for what actually is, suggest for Proust " la seule réalité intéressante." His remarks here anticipate the passage in *Le Temps retrouvé* where he will discuss the metaphor and the fundamental fallacy of Realism: " Ce que nous appelons la réalité est un certain rapport entre ces sensations et ces souvenirs qui nous entourent simultanément—rapport que supprime une simple vision cinématographique, laquelle s'éloigne par là d'autant plus du vrai qu'elle prétend se borner à lui—rapport unique que l'écrivain doit retrouver pour en enchaîner à jamais dans sa phrase les deux termes différents." [78]

Other writers who value primitive impulses and the personal vision have decried all craftsmanship in art. Many twentieth-century writers, particularly the Surrealists, have advocated almost completely spontaneous expression. Not so Proust. To give exact artistic form to a sensation implies for him arduous work. He says of Noailles's poem: ". . . en présence d'une sensation pourtant si fugace qu'on sent que l'artiste a dû être obligé de la recréer mille fois en lui pour prolonger les instants de la pose et pouvoir achever sa toile d'après nature, une des plus étonnantes réussites, le chef-d'œuvre peut-être, de l'' impressionisme' littéraire." [79]

Repelled or merely amused by Proust's cloying flattery to the aristocratic poetess, one is tempted to pass too quickly over his observations upon her works. They deserve close scrutiny, for here and there we may catch very interesting glimpses of Proust's concept of art and of the artist and intimations of the esthetic theories he will eventually develop.

Maurice Barrès

Marcel Proust's contacts with Barrès can be traced as far back as lycée days at Condorcet. There, Maurice Barrès was the object of a veritable cult. His so-called dandyism, which was scandalizing the bourgeois,[80] endeared him to young men ten years his junior who dreamed of an unashamed "cultivation of the ego" as they listened to

[78] *Le Temps retrouvé*, II, 35 ff.

[79] *Correspondance générale*, II, 238.

[80] In the preface to the 1904 edition of *Un Homme libre*, Barrès remembers with exultation the furor his work first caused: " Ceux qui ne connurent jamais l'ivresse de déplaire ne peuvent imaginer les divines satisfactions de ma vingt-cinquième année: j'ai scandalisé. Des gens se mettaient à cause de mes livres en fureur. Leur sottise me crevait de bonheur."

the languid laments of *Un Homme libre*.[81] When young Gregh exhibited the autograph of Barrès he had acquired at an auction, his classmates were tremendously impressed. If Proust's admiration was any less uncritical than the others', it is because of the pangs he suffered upon reading the apocryphal interview with Renan. Barrès's irreverence shocked Proust, who valued among his dearest possessions the bound volumes of Renan's works.

Proust soon met Barrès. One of his school friends, Léon Yeatman, had an uncle who had political affiliations with the young deputy from Nancy. This gentleman prevailed upon Barrès to come to his home for the purpose of introducing Barrès's young admirers. Proust has recorded at least twice the emotions of a young man when he meets a celebrated writer. Recollections of Barrès must have their part in the picture of Bergotte and that of the writer in *Jean Santeuil*. This book brings back to life the little band of young men in love with literature. As Proust was beginning to forsake their company to frequent the Parisian drawing rooms, he had many opportunities to view Barrès at close range. The world of *tout-Paris* was small and exclusive. Proust was going to encounter Barrès in it for the rest of his life. The two were always on very affable terms. But Proust always maintained an attitude of marked deference, never lost his schoolboy respect. And Barrès was always condescending, never seeing in this man whose destiny was to be so much greater than his own, anything more than "our little Proust."

In view of Proust's eccentric, excessive manners, Barrès can scarcely be blamed for an attitude which he shared with Gide, Anatole France, and others who knew Proust in those years. In many ways it seems a privilege not to have known Proust personally! Barrès summed up the general impression when he remarked one day to Benjamin Crémieux that, although he liked Proust well enough, "il y avait sur toute sa personne quelque chose de 'bouffe' qui empêchait de le prendre au sérieux." [82] Moreover, Proust could be extremely importune, as could testify the ladies upon whom he would later call at outlandish hours to get specific details of garments worn many years before. He, so much attached to social niceties, refused to obey the rules of small talk. Anyone who has been cornered at a social gathering by an over-serious young man intent upon obtaining advice on profound or technical matters can understand how tiresome Proust must have been. Jacques-Emile Blanche recalls that Proust "avait la maladresse de l'éperonner [Barrès] sans répit pour obtenir une précision sur un texte, que Barrès lui aurait

[81] "Les jeunes gens ne peuvent se douter de ce qu'avait été Barrès pour ma génération." Fernand Gregh, "Barrès et Proust," *Revue de Paris*, November, 1951, p. 64.

[82] Crémieux, *Du Côté de chez Marcel Proust* (Lemarget, 1929), p. 82.

plutôt demandée." "Insistance," says Blanche, "trait particulier d'une race dont Proust avait l'énergie, la persévérance inébranlable." [83]

During the winter season in Paris, at the fabulous residence of Comte Robert de Montesquiou, at Mme Madeleine Lemaire's, where Reynaldo Hahn would sing, at the studio of Jacques-Emile Blanche, at Mme de Noailles's dinner parties, Proust and Barrès were often in the same company. They met too at Aix and Evian, at the fashionable watering places and beaches, wherever high society moved in the summer. From 1903 on, they were exchanging polite notes, post cards, the books that they wrote. Proust invited Barrès to his parties and musical afternoons. Documents indicate a desultory and somewhat formal friendship lasting throughout the "belle époque." Contacts became rarer as Proust took to his bed and Barrès became more involved in politics. But from time to time a note indicates that Proust had not lost touch entirely with Barrès and wished to be remembered by him. He was confident that he could count on Barrès's friendship. When, in 1913, he was thinking of Grasset as a likely publisher for his book, he wrote René Blum that if a recommendation from a man "d'âge" would be useful, he was sure Barrès would oblige him.[84] After the war, when Proust emerged from his sickroom obscurity, the two grew closer again. Along with Régnier, Léon Daudet, Bergson, and other friends, Barrès sought to have Proust decorated, and urged him to present himself for the Academy. Throughout their lifelong association these two men never failed to greet each other with the correct gesture, and whatever antagonism or lack of sympathy they may have felt toward each other must be sought behind exquisite urbaneness.

Antagonism and lack of sympathy there surely were. As men of ideas and letters, they were often at serious odds. In the matter of principles, they seem never to have thought alike.

The Dreyfus case was the most severe test for their polite intercourse. The question that threw the whole country into two warring camps mobilized both men and set them one against the other. Barrès's decision not to champion the cause of Dreyfus was a bitter blow to the "groupe du *Banquet*." We can infer their reaction from Léon Blum's moving account in his *Souvenirs sur l'affaire* of how he had gone to Barrès to beg him to awaken the national conscience to the monstrous judicial error and was turned away: "Cette lettre tomba sur moi comme un deuil. Quelque chose était brisé, fini; une des avenues de ma jeunesse était close . . . le drame Barrès fut pour moi le plus pathétique." [85] Blum and his friends—"un certain nombre de jeunes juifs, entre lesquels M. Proust"—

[83] Blanche, *Mes Modèles*, p. 98.
[84] Léon Pierre-Quint, *Comment parut "Du Côté de chez Swann"* (Kra, 1930), p. 35.
[85] Gallimard, 1935, pp. 88-89.

were subsequently accused of having publicly manifested against Barrès. Proust denied his association, but only much later and then not publicly. One is not surprised that Barrès found somewhat lame Proust's excuse that a public rectification would have involved the distasteful necessity of pointing out that he was not Jewish.[86] Barrès, who always advertised himself as the leader of youth, knew that his action in the Dreyfus case might disqualify him for the position. The young men of the review found it difficult to take a clear-cut stand which would repudiate Barrès completely. Robert Dreyfus tells us that they remained fundamentally loyal to Barrès: "Barrès connaissait, de longue date, l'admiration que lui avait toujours vouée notre petit groupe du *Banquet*. . . . Admiration assez réfléchie, assez ferme pour lui être restée fidèle,—il le savait bien,— même en des temps fort troublés, pendant les années de véritable guerre civile où nous aurions pu être tentés de ne voir en lui qu'un implacable adversaire." [87] Proust appears more sorrowful than angry with Barrès. At the time of Dreyfus's second trial, Proust wrote his mother from Evian, "Dans le même *Echo* il y a un Lemaître bien troublant comme d'ailleurs le Barrès du verdict aussi médiocre que celui que je t'avais donné était beau, mais d'une apparente sincérité, d'une conviction qui me désole." [88] Curious testimony to the hold Barrès had on this generation!

Barrès's conduct in connection with the Affair brought out traits of character that still today embarrass his admirers. The phrase in *Scènes et doctrines*: "Dreyfus, c'est un champ de bataille où un Français né de sa terre et de ses morts doit accepter le défi des naturalisés et des étrangers" [89] indicates his stand and the measure of his responsibility that this affair, which should have remained only the question of a single man's guilt, flared into a national conflagration involving anti-Semitism and antimilitarism. Barrès was present on the Champ de Mars to see Dreyfus publicly disgraced. His evocation of the scene, "spectacle plus excitant que la guillotine fichée dans les pavés," as well as the other scene at Rennes when Dreyfus entered the courtroom, attest to an ugly delight in observing pain. In this "amateur de sensations fortes," as Albert Thibaudet called him, we see the curious mutation of a taste for blood into a political principle.[90]

Admiration is probably the rarest feeling that the life of Proust inspires in us. From boyhood a sycophant, excessive and oily in his dealings with his social betters, he lacked, one would say, all notion of personal dignity.

[86] Dreyfus, p. 177.
[87] *Ibid.*, p. 174.
[88] Proust, *Correspondance avec sa mère* (Plon, 1953), p. 114.
[89] Barrès, *Scènes et doctrines du nationalisme* (F. Juven, 1902), p. 158.
[90] As early as the Nancy platform, when Barrès was presenting himself as a "socialist" candidate, the essential elements of fascism are contained in his philosophy.

Yet we must make exception for his behavior in connection with the Dreyfus case. Whether because of loyalty to his mother's race—or for whatever reason—for once in his life Proust's backbone stiffened. He manfully took a stand at the risk of unpopularity (nothing more dreadful to Proust) among his titled and elegant friends, dared talk back even to Robert de Montesquiou, whose direct gaze could turn people to stone! As his letters from Evian to his mother show, he engaged himself promptly in the pro-Dreyfus campaign. He worked close to Anatole France, serving him as go-between with influential salons, such as Mme Straus's. Overflowing with respect and devotion to France, he could not help making the bitter reference to Barrès we have cited before: "Vous vous êtes mêlé à la vie publique . . . ni comme Chateaubriand, ni comme Barrès, non pas pour vous faire un nom. . . ." [91] Social relations between Proust and Barrès were strained if not severed altogether for a time, since in most salons "Dreyfusards" did not meet "Nationalistes." It is gratifying to know that at least on one occasion Proust's feelings ran so high as to make a direct retort to Barrès. In a laudatory article on the "grand poète, la comtesse de Noailles," whose intimate friend he had recently become, Barrès had introduced a subtle barb aimed at her supposed Dreyfusism. Referring to the famous verse of La Fontaine on Fouquet, justly condemned, Barrès had declared the poetess was wrong in thinking that "C'était être innocent que d'être malheureux." When next Proust and Barrès met, Proust remarked quite sharply that "c'était être innocent que d'être malheureux," and moreover "c'était malheureux d'être innocent quand on était condamné." Barrès merely laughed and said, "Que signifie cette brusque explosion de Dreyfusisme?" [92]

Proust was not given to many such outbursts, and a polite reconciliation soon took place between the two men. "Une solennelle réconciliation ce soir chez les Noailles, entre moi et Barrès, à qui je n'ai pas mâché de dures vérités, politiques et morales. Mais il les a fort bien prises et a été très gentil. Et successivement, pour Rouvier, pour Picquart, pour Labori, m'a donné des excuses—non valables d'ailleurs—de sa conduite." [93] The letter of condolence that Barrès wrote on the occasion of Mme Proust's death further assuaged Proust's hurt feelings. He wrote Barrès in 1906 that he would like all the Dreyfusards to understand the "délicatesse infinie et la bonté" of Barrès's heart.[94] Personal fondness for Barrès acted as a check on Proust's indignation. At times, though, not trusting his own pen, he conveys his compliments via a third person. To the

[91] See p. 12, n. 21.
[92] Proust, *Lettres à Bibesco* (Lausanne: Clairefontaine, 1949), p. 90.
[93] *Correspondance avec sa mère*, p. 285.
[94] Elisabeth de Gramont (Duchesse de Clermont-Tonnerre), "Quelques Lettres inédites de Marcel Proust à Maurice Barrès," *Écrits de Paris*, January, 1951, p. 103.

Comtesse Noailles he wrote: "Barrès a été bien courageux et noble l'autre jour à la Chambre!" Proust cannot refrain from adding, "Dites-le-lui, et que je ne lui écris pas, parce qu'il faudrait que j'ajoute immédiatement que Dreyfus est tout de même innocent et que, malgré ma grande pitié pour le général Mercier, c'est une fameuse canaille." [95]

Nothing in Barrès's political philosophy could appeal to Proust. Allusions to the "Nationaliste" program in Proust's letters carry unmistakable indications of irony or lack of sympathy. "Quant au nationalisme intégral, j'avoue que je suis extraordinairement peu ferré là-dessus." [96] He praised Lauris for his article on Barrès in *La Nouvelle Revue*, especially for "toute la page sur la mauvaise influence de Barrès" and the "critique de la théorie du déracinement." [97]

Did political and ideological differences leave intact Proust's appreciation for Barrès as a writer? In spite of his "profonde antipathie" for what he had felt was his "mauvais cœur" in the Dreyfus Affair he seems to have always kept "une immense admiration pour le talent de Barrès." [98] Knowing Proust's manner, we must not take very seriously the hyperbolic praise he heaped upon the writer who was also a friend. Let us scrutinize it carefully, nevertheless, to observe what aspects of Barrès Proust found fit to smother with flowers. Proust's first interest in any author was the opportunity he afforded the reader to see with a new pair of eyes, to acquire a new sensitivity. Barrès's vision is what interested him chiefly. Particularly his vision of nature. What characterizes his landscapes? "Une certaine horizontalité d'eau où traîne un reflet, c'est ce qui caractérise le plus profondément vos tableaux." [99] Every artist paints a scene according to his own subjective eye. Proust noted in Barrès's art certain changes in tone, certain exquisite colorations which are his alone.[100] Comparing her work to Barrès's, Proust wrote to Anna de Noailles: "Il est même inouï de penser à quel point votre admirable Venise diffère de son admirable Venise, votre admirable Bruges de son admirable Bruges, alors que l'image si particulière qu'il avait donnée de ces deux villes semblait devoir commander pendant si longtemps les sensibilités littéraires. Et les commandera en effet, sauf cette exception et ce miracle d'une vue de génie qui s'interpose." [101] We have in this letter

[95] The allusion is to Barrès's speech in the Chambre, July 13, 1906, at the time of Dreyfus's rehabilitation. *Correspondance générale*, II, 152.

[96] *Ibid.*, IV, 191.

[97] *À Un Ami*, pp. 57-58.

[98] *Correspondance générale*, II, 66. Barrès's grief at the death of his nephew has made the tender Proust now feel that he was wrong in ever attributing to Barrès a "mauvais cœur."

[99] Gramont, p. 104.

[100] Proust, letter to Barrès. See Barrès, *Mes Cahiers* (Plon, 1935), IX, 162.

[101] *Correspondance générale*, II, 122.

a prefiguration of Proust's esthetic as it will be elaborated in *Le Temps retrouvé*.

All the artist's talent is deployed in recording the inner vision exactly. Exactness and "inevitability" are touchstones of Proustian criticism. Thus he praised in Barrès his "lignes délicieuses et justes; Barrès avec deux mots en dit plus que moi."[102] Proust would bend long over a literary passage to determine what stylistic procedures conveyed this new vision of things—diction, tenses, syntax, juxtaposition of observation and imagination. Just as in Flaubert he had observed a notable use of the imperfect tense, in Barrès he noted a "brusque emploi du présent de l'indicatif, là où on met généralement l'imparfait et le parfait."[103] Proust did not rest until he knew the mechanics of an author's style well enough to imitate it perfectly. Of his *Pastiches*, Barrès once declared that Proust had found in them "la formule de la critique fondée sur ce que, selon l'avis de Buffon, il n'y a pas lieu de distinguer le fond de la forme."[104] This is probably the only astute comment Barrès ever made on Proust's work.

Proust's admiration is greater for Barrès the artist than for Barrès the theorist, even in esthetic theory. He could not follow Barrès in what we nowadays call engaged art: "Dès le début de la guerre M. Barrès avait dit que l'artiste . . . doit avant tout servir la gloire de sa patrie. Mais il ne peut la servir qu'en étant artiste, c'est-à-dire qu'à condition au moment où il étudie les lois de l'Art, institue ses expériences et fait ses découvertes, aussi délicates que celles de la Science, de ne pas penser à autre chose—fût-ce à la patrie—qu'à la vérité qui est devant lui."[105] There are several such documents which show that in matters of esthetic theory Barrès and Proust held widely divergent views. It is the earlier Barrès, the idol of the young esthetes, that appealed most to Proust and with whom we can detect a certain affinity.

Germaine Brée[106] and, before her, Ramon Fernandez[107] have studied rather closely the resemblances between Proust and the Barrès of the *Culte du moi* series. Both point out in Barrès certain tendencies and themes that Proust will exploit, certain viewpoints and modes of expression that in Proust will be emphasized to the point of being considered peculiarly his. *Un Homme libre* contains in embryo remarkably much of *À La Recherche du temps perdu*.

Temperamentally young Barrès had much in common with Proust.

[102] Gramont, p. 100.
[103] *Correspondance générale*, II, 121.
[104] *À Un Ami*, p. 171.
[105] *Le Temps retrouvé*, II, 34.
[106] "Marcel Proust et Maurice Barrès," *Romanic Review*, XL (April, 1949), 93-105.
[107] *Maurice Barrès* (Ed. du Livre Moderne, 1943).

One thinks one is listening to Proust as Barrès says of himself: "Je penche quelquefois à me développer dans le sens de l'énervement; névropathe et délicat, j'aurais enregistré les plus menues disgrâces de la vie."[108] Fernandez comments apropos of this statement: "C'est chez l'un et chez l'autre, même atonie musculaire, même neurasthénie, mêmes 'menues disgrâces' d'une sensibilité sans défenses, et aussi, disons-le, même froideur profonde et désespérée sous les aiguillons intermittents de l'émotion."[109] Only a strong will pulled Barrès out of the path of a Proust.

In view of Barrès's prestige during Proust's formative years, it is quite natural to seek a prefiguration of Proust's study of the ego in Barrès's first books. Barrès had already gazed "with reverted eye inwards," trying to determine the nature of the ego and define its relation to the non-ego. Recording the fluctuations and the multiple aspects of his personality, he had become profoundly aware of the insufficiencies of classic psychology. Barrès, before Proust, had described the *intermittances* of the heart and of the personality in general: "Un état de conscience ne peut naître en nous que par la mort de l'individu que nous étions hier."[110] A person is a collection of beings, his states of consciousness common property shared with his ancestors and his contemporaries, belonging no more to him than to anyone else. The conception of personality that led him to think of himself in terms of the province and the nation would lead Proust to the universal—"c'est dans une trame universelle que nos individualités sont taillées."[111] If Barrès jealously protected his ego from the "Barbarians" who threatened to come between himself and his consciousness of self, if Proust struggled against the trivial pleasures of social life which distracted him from his study, it is because both conceived of the individual personality as naturally fluid and free, and deplored its congealing into the molds that routine and convention tend to set upon it.

The "moi" so defined is all-important. Its limitations define the world and the nature of things. Barrès's "courte monographie réaliste" takes the subjective and relativistic point of view characteristic of Proust: "La réalité varie avec chacun de nous. . . ."[112] Persons and places have significance only as re-created in the individual consciousness. This becomes clear as we watch them analyze love. The loved one is considered an object, a wax figure created by the lover and fashioned according to his sentimental and erotic impulses. Places, too, polarize sentiments and emotions, possess no autonomous existence of significance. In this connection the passages in which both authors speak of Venice should be studied

[108] *Un Homme libre* (Perrin, 1889), p. 287.
[109] Fernandez, p. 77.
[110] *Le Jardin de Bérénice* (Plon, 1920), p. 181.
[111] Proust, *La Bible d'Amiens* (Mercure de France, 1904), p. 18.
[112] *Sous L'Oeil des barbares* (Plon, 1927), p. 51.

carefully. Note Barrès's private Venice: "Mes souvenirs, rapidement déformés par mon instinct, me présentèrent une Venise qui n'existe nulle part. . . . Et cette cité abstraite, bâtie pour mon usage personnel, se déroulait devant mes yeux clos, hors du temps et de l'espace. . . . Cette synthèse, dont j'étais l'artisan, me fit paraître bien mesquine la Venise bornée où se réjouissent les artistes et les touristes." [113]

Subjective re-creation by recourse to memory is the keystone of Proust's esthetic edifice. Barrès knew that the inner vision of things, alone, was real and beautiful. But happier than Proust, he knew how to transfer his impressions to re-create his scene on the spot, possess it in its presence, so to speak. Proust's failure to synchronize his visions in this fashion is clearly confessed in the episode of the Martinville steeples [114] and accounts for the emphasis he placed on the *mémoire involontaire.* This difference suggests an important cleavage between these personalities which seem at this point so close. Proust, with infinite patience and humility, had to await his visitations. He had to reconcile himself to an altogether passive role, an anxious vigil. Barrès, on the other hand, soon left off contemplating his ego to turn it into an active and militant force.

To justify his egoism, Barrès extended it to include province and race. The languid Narcissus was also a fledgling politician. Identifying the ego with a social group commits one almost inevitably to participation and action. Barrès's development was perfectly natural, obvious already to any attentive reader of *Un Homme libre.* Health permitting, would Proust also have moved toward the market place and the arena? In view of his activities in the Dreyfus struggle, such a supposition is not without some foundation. When Proust took to his bed to write his novel, it was clearly an act of retirement from the world, a renunciation bitterly hard for Proust.

If Proust could not participate in the affairs of men, he could from a vantage point observe the human spectacle and meditate undisturbed upon fundamental problems. Within the cork-lined walls that kept the noise of the market place from being too distracting, he could give his attention to his memories and sensations. Barrès left his self-contemplative youth behind him. But Proust, true to the teachings of Simon and his "brothers," continued the patient researches and analyses of his emotions which we know in *À La Recherche du temps perdu.* The flashes of intuition that came to Barrès were left by the wayside: "Partout où il passe, il se comporte en placier de lui-même: il dépose, ici et là, un échantillon

[113] *Un Homme libre,* p. 221. Compare with Proust's treatment of Venice, particularly in *Le Temps retrouvé,* II. For complete references, see Raoul Celly, *Répertoire des thèmes* (Gallimard, 1935), p. 332.

[114] *Du Côté de chez Swann,* I.

et fait comme s'il avait dit: 'Je repasserai plus tard.'"[115] But Proust in his bed developed and unified them into a powerful synthesis.

Barrès was not unaware of the task he had left undone. "Je considère avec affolement combien la vie est pleine de fragments de bonheur que je ne saurai jamais harmoniser, et d'indications vers rien du tout."[116] How ironical that he could not recognize that Proust's long tarrying in adolescent estheticism had led him ultimately to the goal Barrès and his heroes had set for themselves! The integration of art and metaphysics, the insight into human nature and the meaning of existence, the recipe for the perfect life—all that which is longed for but never attained in *Un Homme libre* is explicitly stated in *Temps perdu* for generations of twenty-year-olds forever to study and to follow. But for Barrès, Proust could never be more than "un conteur arabe dans la loge de la portière! Peu importe le canevas sur lequel Proust brode ses arabesques, tout ressemble aux fleurs, aux oiseaux des boîtes de rahat-loukoum."[117]

Henri de Régnier

Henri de Régnier merits a place along with Anatole France, Barrès, Montesquiou, and the Comtesse de Noailles in the gallery of Proust's dear friends and masters. A unique place actually, for the doubts and differences, complicated by a desire to please, which render suspect some of Proust's judgments of the others, are absent here. For Régnier, Proust apparently felt only a frank admiration and a genuine fondness.

He was attracted to him early. One of Proust's first literary essays is an article (1892) on the volume of poems entitled *Tel qu'en songe*.[118] *Les Plaisirs et les jours* (1896) bears a marked affinity to Régnier's *La Canne de Jaspe* and contains an epigraph of some verses from a poem in *Sites*.[119] Before 1900 Proust had met Régnier and was inviting him to his receptions. One of the Lemoine pastiches (1909) (one of the two best ones, according to Proust)[120] was devoted to Régnier. If Proust mimicked the mannerisms of the poet and protested against his tolerance of mediocre writers,[121] there is no evidence of deflection from his basic loyalty. Régnier, for his part, appreciated Proust's esteem and recognized his admirer's own talents. Letters Proust wrote in 1920 frequently allude to Régnier's efforts to win a decoration for Proust or a seat in the

[115] Fernandez, p. 135.
[116] *Un Homme libre*, pp. 268-69.
[117] Blanche, p. 117.
[118] Proust, *Chroniques* (Gallimard, 1927), pp. 175-76.
[119] Régnier, *Premiers Poèmes* (Mercure de France, 1898), p. 127.
[120] *À Un Ami*, p. 244.
[121] *Ibid.*, p. 174.

Academy.[122] By this time Proust's own literary greatness was generally recognized. Notwithstanding, his deference to Régnier remained constant. With remarkable modesty, the author of *À La Recherche du temps perdu* declared, "Certes, en rien je ne me compare à lui, je serais aussi incapable de sa *Double Maîtresse* que de son *Bon Plaisir*." [123]

Proust's remarks on *Tel qu'en songe* constitute not only a judgment of Régnier's poetry but an indication of what Proust considered fundamental poetic values. In two short pages of praise he states his position regarding appreciation of poetry, *poésie pure*, and the superior intelligence of poets. His attitude on all three matters derives from the basic suspicion of the intellect intrinsic in all Proust's esthetic views.[124]

To appreciate poetry, Proust begins, one needs neither erudition nor intelligence. A salutatory opening, modest and a bit coquettish perhaps for one who is about to write a review, but clearly indicative that Proust placed the faculty for appreciating poetry somewhere outside the intellect. Most poetry, he claims, has extraneous material which offers entertainment to those incapable of enjoying the essentially poetic. In Régnier, however, there is no eloquence or rhetoric for such readers to seize upon, nothing but "un infini bruissant et bleuâtre, reflétant l'éternité du ciel, vierge comme la mer, sans un vestige humain, sans un débris terrestre." Have we not here a renewed pledge to the Symbolist effort to attain the absolute and an anticipation of the famous debate over *poésie pure* as it developed with Valéry and Bremond? Note that both in *Jean Santeuil* and in *Du Côté de chez Swann* Proust tells of his early ponderings over the problem of the essence of poetry. Bloch's assertion that the beauty of verse was apart from its meaning had greatly disturbed the young reader, "fou de la poésie." The role of the intelligence vis-à-vis a work of art was a question that Proust never solved quite to his satisfaction. We find him worrying much later that the *Rohstoff* might be superior to a work polished and perfected at great pains.[125] Here he asks himself, "Si une telle poésie n'est pas œuvre d'intelligence, comment oserons-nous la juger divine . . . ?" His solution is the Symbolist one, harking back to Kantian distinctions between *Vernunft* and *Verstand*: "Au-dessus de ce qu'on appelle généralement intelligence, les philosophes cherchent à saisir une raison supérieure une et infinie comme le sentiment, à la fois objet et instrument de leurs méditations. C'est un peu de cette raison, de ce senti-

[122] *Correspondance générale*, III, 81, 83, 228; *Lettres à la N.R.F.* (Gallimard, 1932), p. 113.

[123] *Correspondance générale*, II, 208-9.

[124] Note particularly the Sainte-Beuve essay (*Contre Sainte-Beuve* [Gallimard, 1954]), written a few years after the review of Régnier's volume, which represents Proust's most concentrated attack on the intelligence.

[125] *Correspondance générale*, III, 139.

ment mystérieux et profond des choses que *Tel qu'en songe* réalise ou présente."

Already in this little essay, written when Proust was twenty-one, we have the basic esthetic ideas which Proust will elaborate as his final message to the world in the second volume of *Le Temps retrouvé*. The high seriousness here contrasts with the buffoonery of the commentary on Régnier in *Mondanité et mélomanie de Bouvard et Pécuchet*. These two fools dispose of the poet with no hesitation: "Quant à Henri de Régnier c'est un fumiste ou un fou, nulle autre alternative." Their judgment is made up of tag ends of the commonplaces of contemporary critics: "Du reste, dites tant que vous voudrez que ces lignes inégales sont des vers, je me refuse à y voir autre chose que de la prose, et sans signification encore!" [126]

The pastiche on Régnier, which appeared in 1909, may be studied as a concise analysis of Régnier's prose style. Proust was extremely fond of that opulent and at the same time ironic manner, so characteristic of the period and of the sort of thing Proust himself was given to in his early writing. Two years before his pastiche he had written to the Comtesse de Noailles: "Le jardin d'Henri de Régnier, Dieu sait si je l'aime. C'est peut-être le premier que j'aie connu; chaque année écoulée me l'a rendu plus admirable, et il ne s'en passe guère où je ne retourne plusieurs fois le visiter, soit chez M. d'Amercœur, M. de Heurteleure ou la princesse de Termiane, plus souvent à Pont-aux-Belles, et jamais alors sans pousser ma pointe de pèlerinage jusqu'au Fresnay. Quant à Bas-le-Pré, dès que, encore loin du jardin, je reconnais dans le ciel pluvieux ses tourelles pointues, j'éprouve un peu du tressaillement qui saisit M. de Portebize quand les lui décrit M. d'Oriocourt." [127] The acuity of observation and the familiarity with Régnier's stories indicated here show how well prepared Proust was to counterfeit some pages of that author. The text itself demonstrates a remarkable mastery of Régnier's fundamental procedures.

The proper names are immediately familiar: Hermas is taken directly from the *Trèfle noir*; M. de Séryeuse is quite typical of Régnier by its aristocratic air (like M. de Sérences) and by its punning character (like M. d'Amercœur). The introductory sentence, "Le diamant ne me plaît guère," recalls Régnier's first-person beginnings, by which he haughtily measures the distance between himself as narrator and the events of his narrative. The divagations on precious stones, set in motion by reference to the Lemoine fabrication, strike a characteristic note, as do all the baroque and costly properties that Proust uses to set his stage. As in many Régnier stories, the narrator begins by describing his arrival before

[126] *Les Plaisirs et les jours*, pp. 100-101.
[127] *Correspondance générale*, II, 232-33.

an unknown château, very *vieille France* with its dilapidated beauties, its statues, peacocks, doves, its graveled walks, and its gardens. It evokes all those palaces of Régnier, surrounded by mystery and portentious signs, where sounds and shadows excite wild fancies: "Agatisé par sa lumière, l'Hermès du seuil s'obscurcissait plus de sa disparition qu'il n'eût fait de son absence. Successif et ambigu, le visage marmoréen vivait. Un sourire semblait allonger en forme de caducée les lèvres expiatrices." Proust is imitating the many descriptive passages in Régnier like the following: "Leur reflet se métallisait dans une eau calme où celui des statues semblait se dissoudre à demi, se fondre en une sorte d'aspect d'outre vie, moins leur image que leur ombre, car toute eau est un peu magique et, si elle est tout à fait tranquille, on ne sait pas ce qui y peut dormir." [128] Like Régnier, Proust has employed odors, luminosities, and undefined noises to intensify his atmosphere of irreality and magic.

Proust's ending of the pastiche, where he transforms the Lemoine diamond into a blob of nasal mucus, is a masterpiece of buffoonery, an intrusion of revolting realism that would certainly delight the author of *La Double Maîtresse* and *Le Bon Plaisir*. Régnier's irony frequently led him to such jovial incongruities. In the latter novel, the scene describing the glorious and majestic passage of the King of France through a small town closes on a view of the departing horses: "Les croupes solides luisaient. L'une d'elles laissa tomber un crottin doré comme une médaille à quelque effigie souveraine." [129]

The tour de force we applaud most is Proust's capture of Régnier's syntactical peculiarities. He employs a sumptuous and complex sentence to burlesque what would be traced by Régnier's pen. The stacking of adjectives, catachresis, and zeugma are monkeyshines to delight readers of Régnier, and, for that matter, of most Symbolist authors. The perilous balancing of epithets is integrated into an elaborate structure of juxtaposed clauses, with matched pronouns and crisscrossed antecedents. Frequent repetition and an unstinting use of *que* and *qui* are necessary to balance the parts and complete the scheme. There is no doubt that Proust was consciously using these devices, for, in answer to a friend's concern lest Régnier might be offended by the pastiche, he wrote: "Il n'y a pourtant rien qui puisse le mécontenter. Il doit bien savoir qu'il enchevêtre les pronoms puisque certainement cette syntaxe néo saint-simonienne est voulue chez lui et quant à ce qu'il répète plusieurs fois la même chose il doit bien le savoir aussi." [130] Proust's assumption was

[128] *La Canne de Jaspe* (Mercure de France, 1922), p. 136.
[129] *Le Bon Plaisir* (Mercure de France, 1922), pp. 117-18.
[130] *À Un Ami*, p. 170.

soon substantiated by a complimentary letter from Régnier declaring that he found the pastiche a very close imitation indeed.[131]

The stylistic features Proust parodies so well in Régnier are not different from those of his own early manner: complicated syntactical balances, parentheses, technical terms of architecture and decoration, introduced not so much for reasons of pedantic exactitude as for their mysterious and poetic effects.[132] The kinship between *Les Plaisirs et les jours* and *La Canne de Jaspe* is remarkably close. In addition to stylistic similarities, the themes and subjects treated bespeak common preoccupations; a hothouse atmosphere pervades the two works. What France wrote in his preface to *Les Plaisirs et les jours* applies equally well to *La Canne de Jaspe.*

The family resemblance to many other works of the period, plus the fact that Régnier's work (1897) appeared after Proust's (1896), has discouraged thinking along lines of specific influence. Jean Mouton declares: "Mais on ne peut parler d'influence; *Les Plaisirs et les jours* . . . parurent avant les premiers textes en prose de cet auteur. C'est donc, à l'origine, simple parenté entre les deux esprits."[133] This statement is not quite exact. A good part of *La Canne de Jaspe* had appeared prior to Proust's publication date. *Contes à soi-même* had appeared separately in 1894.[134] There remains the question of the exact dates of composition, a question that cannot be readily answered. Proust's indications are contradictory,[135] but it seems likely that some pieces were written several years before others. Without evidence to the contrary, we may assume the same is true of Régnier. Unfortunately I cannot ascertain whether the two authors were acquainted personally early enough to make likely an exchange of ideas or of manuscripts.[136] At any rate, it seems too much to say that one cannot speak of an influence. It is quite possible that Proust's first book owes direct inspiration to Henri de Régnier.

[131] *Ibid.*, p. 172.

[132] See Jean Mouton, *Le Style de Marcel Proust* (Corrêa, 1948), pp. 43-44.

[133] *Ibid.*, p. 43.

[134] See Robert Honnert, *Henri de Régnier* (Ed. de la Nouvelle Revue Critique, 1923), p. 31.

[135] In his preface to *Les Plaisirs et les jours,* Proust speaks of certain stories being composed when he was only twenty. In a letter to Vaudoyer, written much later, he says seventeen. (*Correspondance générale,* IV, 38.)

[136] The earliest document I know attesting to a personal acquaintance is tentatively dated 1899. (See *Correspondance générale,* I, 92, and Philip Kolb, *La Correspondance de Marcel Proust* [Urbana: University of Illinois Press, 1949], p. 439.)

CHAPTER TWO

Classmates and Companions

Members of the little clan at Condorcet and collaborators on the *Banquet* remained Proust's friends for life. They watched the progress of one another's careers with loyal interest, and offered advice and kindly criticism. In following several of these literary friendships we come upon interesting testimony concerning Proust's personality and his esthetic principles. We observe his growth and spiritual development through personal contacts. And we glean provocative appreciations and estimations of the works of his friends who were also writers of distinction.

Robert Dreyfus

Robert Dreyfus, better known in the field of history than in belles-lettres, is remembered particularly as the biographer of Gobineau. But to readers of Proust, Dreyfus is of greatest importance as a memorialist. His *Souvenirs sur Marcel Proust* gives us the testimony of a close friend who remembered Proust from childhood when they played together in the park along the Champs-Elysées. From the age of fifteen on, Dreyfus began collecting letters from Proust, never throwing one of them away. They have appeared in the *Souvenirs* and also in the fourth volume of the *Correspondance générale.*

In the Allée de l'Alcazar the two lads talked of literature. Marcel, two years older, initiated Robert into the beauties of French poetry: "Racine, Hugo, Musset, Lamartine, Baudelaire chantaient dejà dans sa prodigieuse mémoire poétique, et je me souviens d'avoir connu par lui le nom de Leconte de Lisle." [1]

At Condorcet their admiration turned to the "moderns." Proust found fault with one of their teachers, M. Dupré, whose appreciation for the new literature was not without reservations: "Il est vrai qu'il connaît Dierx et Leconte de Lisle (les œuvres). Mais à quoi ça te servira-t-il de t'entendre parler d'auteurs modernes par un homme qui ne les aimera qu'avec trop de réserves?" [2]

Although Dreyfus rarely saw Proust after the year of the *Banquet*

[1] Dreyfus, *Souvenirs sur Marcel Proust,* p. 16.
[2] *Correspondance générale,* IV, 171.

(1892-93), he kept in touch by lengthy correspondence, much of which concerned their writing. Here is what Proust wrote about Dreyfus's first published essay: "J'ai reçu ce matin–je ne sais si c'est toi qui me les as fait envoyer–*les Essais*. Et j'ai lu ces pages délicieuses, d'une extraordinaire élégance, même dans les profondeurs. C'est vraiment tout à fait remarquable. Avec une espèce de curiosité stendhalienne, de goût pour les petits faits sociaux, tu recueilles, assembles, concentres toute la saveur éparse de ton personnage. Et dans l'évocation du système tu es prodigieux. Et de [*sic*] qualités tout autres. Me voici gobinien. Je ne pense qu'à lui." [3] His praise is mingled with the caviling on points of syntax and grammar Proust permitted himself with his friends' writing. Occasionally he is led to general observations transcending the immediate point he is making. An "Art of Writing According to Proust" could be composed from statements such as the following that he made concerning *Quarante-huit; Essais d'histoire contemporaine*: "C'est très bien d'écrire 'selon l'esprit' et de recevoir de lui seul son rythme, mais quelquefois cela nuit un peu à la clarté ou du moins au 'coulant' et sans grande nécessité." [4]

The letters continue down through the years. The most valuable one, perhaps, is one dated 1913 in which Proust speaks of memory and involuntary memory as a leitmotif of his book and in which he defines style: "Le style n'est nullement un enjolivement comme croient certaines personnes, ce n'est même pas une question de technique, c'est–comme la couleur chez les peintres–une qualité de la vision, la révélation de l'univers particulier que chacun de nous voit, et que ne voient pas les autres. Le plaisir que nous donne un artiste, c'est de nous faire connaître un univers de plus." [5]

Daniel Halévy

Proust's letters to Daniel Halévy have never been published, but we can follow their association through letters to others and through books of reminiscences, notably those of Jacques-Emile Blanche and Robert Dreyfus. Their friendship was not without its moments of tension; in fact even as schoolboys they seem to have had their differences.

Young Proust's droll manners and excessive compliments had made him seem odd to his classmates. He could not understand their attitude toward him and imagined all sorts of slights and affronts. His difficulties are recalled in *Jean Santeuil*: "Il ne comprenait pas que ce besoin de sympathie, cette sensibilité maladive et trop fine qui le faisait déborder d'amour à la moindre gentillesse, choquaient comme de l'hypocrisie,

[3] Dreyfus, p. 163.
[4] *Ibid.*, p. 210.
[5] *Ibid.*, p. 292.

agaçaient comme de la pose ces jeunes gens, chez qui l'indifférence d'une nature plus froide se doublait de la dureté de leur âge." [6] Daniel Halévy, in particular, seems to have offended him. He complained bitterly to Dreyfus, who always served them as intermediary or message bearer, and sought from him clarification and reassurance: "As-tu voulu poliment me dire qu'Halévy me trouvait brac et toc?" [7] he questioned suspiciously.

Although Proust was regarded as a queer duck by his classmates and made to suffer accordingly, he was an unqualified success in the drawing room. When Daniel's parents, M. and Mme Ludovic Halévy, asked him to stay for dinner, they and their distinguished guests found Marcel's deportment exquisite: "Un garçon si bien élevé, si respectueux des aînés, s'il effarait un peu, par de pompeuses manières d'une autre époque, de braves dames inaccoutumées au baise-main, aux fleurs et bonbons offerts par un jouvenceau, il les éblouissait par les ressources d'une mémoire jamais en défaut, nourrie de lectures que l'on ne faisait plus." [8]

After the lycée, the members of the clan were scattered in the various schools of Paris: Halévy was learning Arabic at the École des Langues orientales, Proust was at the École des Sciences politiques. The *Banquet* brought them together again. Its title was Halévy's idea. In its second number one could read his article on Friedrich Nietzsche, one of the pioneer studies in France on the German philosopher.

Proust and Halévy gradually drifted apart as the years went on. Their enthusiasm often took them in opposite directions. Halévy developed, for example, a great admiration for Charles Péguy, whose life furnished the subject of one of Halévy's principal biographies. Proust, on the contrary, execrated the author of *Sainte Jeanne*, and if he subscribed to the *Cahiers de la Quinzaine*, it was only to please his former comrade and to let the numbers gather dust in his room. Proust continued to admire Halévy himself without sharing his tastes. Of *Les Trois Croix*, which appeared in the *Débats* in 1914, he wrote his friends enthusiastically: "Avez-vous lu *Les Trois Croix?* A part certains articles purement militaires, c'est la chose [. . . ?] décente que j'ai lu sur la guerre." [9] Proust, to whom "engagement" was basically antipathetic, did not mince words about writers who thought they could help the war effort in writing: "Du reste à part un ou deux, les littérateurs qui en ce moment croient 'servir' en écrivant, parlent bien mal de tout cela. (Il y a des exceptions, avez-vous lu *Les trois Croix*, de Daniel Halévy, dans les *Débats*. . . ." [10]

[6] *Jean Santeuil*, I, 324-25.
[7] *Correspondance générale*, IV, 175.
[8] Blanche, *Mes Modèles*, p. 100.
[9] *À Un Ami*, p. 240.
[10] Lucien Daudet, *Autour De Soixante Lettres de Marcel Proust* (Gallimard, 1929), p. 106.

After the war, Proust took issue with Halévy over his adherence to what Proust considered a false and dangerous literary position. Fifty-four writers, among them Daniel Halévy, had signed a manifesto entitled "Pour un Parti de l'Intelligence," which proclaimed that one of the great missions of the Catholic church had been to protect man from himself, that is, to prevent doubt from attacking reason, thereby maintaining the prestige and dignity of human thought. Proust found the statement flatly absurd. He replied to Halévy: "Personne plus que moi n'admire l'Eglise, mais prendre le contre-pied d'Homais jusqu'à dire qu'elle a été la tutelle des progrès de l'esprit humain, en tous temps, est un peu fort." The proclamation advocated, furthermore, an intellectual federation of Europe and the world under the leadership of victorious France, the seat of culture. Proust retorted to this nonsense: "Proclamer une espèce de 'Frankreich über alles,' gendarme de la littérature de tous les peuples, rôle qu'il eût été plus discret d'attendre que les autres peuples lui confiassent." [11]

Halévy seemed always to be saying the wrong thing. Proust's displeasure was further aroused as he read Halévy's praise of Sainte-Beuve: "Aussi j'ai été désolé quand j'ai vu mon ami Daniel Halévy célébrer Sainte-Beuve comme le plus sûr des guides. Si je ne l'avais assommé de lettres de reproches pour avoir signé le stupide manifeste du parti de l'intelligence, je lui aurais répondu dans un journal." [12] But he found words of praise for Halévy's book on Péguy. Knowing how little Proust cared for the subject, we may assume his compliment is perfunctory. In spite of divergent tastes, the bonds of long-standing friendship remained firm. When Halévy asked Proust to sign the copy of *Sentiments filiaux d'un parricide* that he had carefully preserved for many years, Proust covered the blank pages with reminiscences of their youth together. Halévy gave *Temps perdu* laudatory publicity in the press, which, from his sickbed, Proust gratefully acknowledged.

Fernand Gregh

Fernand Gregh wrote in his brief contribution to *Hommage à Marcel Proust* that he could fill a volume with his souvenirs of Proust. Although he has never done precisely that, he has given us a good number of them in his articles and memoirs. From these, and from the letters to Gregh that have been published, we follow fairly well the course of their friendship. Proust, being two years older than Gregh, was consequently ahead of him at Condorcet, but they became very well acquainted through their collaboration on the *Banquet*. For it Gregh wrote his first critical article,

[11] *Correspondance générale*, IV, 278-79.
[12] *Ibid.*, III, 68.

a study on Paul Desjardins. He praised this poet for moral inspiration and perfection of form. Moreover, in decrying the skepticism and dilettantism in vogue at the time, Desjardins had taken a position with which the *Banquet* was wholly sympathetic.

The group was proud of its lyric poet, Fernand Gregh, and Proust, in particular, sought out his company. He presented him to his parents and invited him to dinner with Bergson. When summer came, Gregh often dined at the Proust-Weil family home in Auteuil. He and Proust would eat in the garden and talk for long hours in the rural quiet. They joined Bizet, Louis de la Salle, Gabriel Trarieux, and Robert de Billy in outings in Normandy and at Les Frémonts, which, with its three "views," is described in *Sodome et Gomorrhe* under the name of La Raspelière.[13] The *Banquet* collaborators did not disband even after the magazine ceased publication. They met to discuss literature and art, and frequently they sang to Gregh's accompaniment at the piano.

Just how close Proust and Gregh were in these years is indicated by the curious story Gregh published under the title of "Mystères." [14] M. René de Messières [15] has called our attention to this work, asserting that in it Gregh is describing one of Proust's famous attacks of *mémoire involontaire*. Messières's assertions were challenged by Mme Gabriel Czoniczer, who, although unconvinced that Gregh's hero is really Proust, agrees that the work contains in germ some ideas (notably that of the involuntary memory) which are fundamental in Proust's own work.[16]

Proust and Gregh, in the years following the *Banquet*, continued to confide in each other concerning their literary projects, requested advice, and complimented each other enthusiastically. On the occasion of Gregh's *Clartés humaines* (1903), Proust addressed to its author one of his exquisitely contrived letters of felicitation which, despite their excessiveness, so enchant their recipients that they can never throw them away. It is to Gregh's credit that he demurred for over fifty years before exhibiting this letter. One wonders, however, if it would not be more seemly to publish without ado all that one possesses from Proust's pen for its documentary value alone, rather than to extract a letter now and then from a pocket near the heart to glorify a forgotten work of one's own. This missive, produced, with a flutter of apologies, for its "valeur esthétique," demonstrates how young Gregh has attained Aristotelian verity in his volume of verse, "ni matérialistement descriptive, ni ab-

[13] Gregh, *L'Age d'or* (Grasset, 1947), p. 165.

[14] *La Revue Blanche*, XI, 259.

[15] "Un Document probable sur le premier état de la pensée de Proust," *Romanic Review*, XXXIII (1942), 113-31.

[16] "Marcel Proust ou Fernand Gregh?" *Ibid.*, XXXV (1944), 232-37.

straitement raisonneuse, mais qui en tout dégage, de la forme même, l'esprit individuel et transcendant qu'il y a en chaque chose. . . ." [17] "Dame," we say with Marotte of the *Précieuses ridicules,* "Je n'ai pas appris, comme vous, la filofie dans le grand Cyre!" But both Proust and Gregh had studied philosophy with Darlu at Condorcet and remembered their lessons well.

When *Clartés* received an unfavorable review in the *Renaissance Latine,* Proust hastened to salve his friend's wounds. Gaston Rageot had, Gregh tells us,[18] originally written great praise of the volume, but, due to the machinations of Anna de Noailles, subsequently turned his article into an "éreintement." Proust, probably not unhappy to take a thrust at Rageot, who had been chosen over himself for the post with the *Renaissance Latine,* treats Rageot's article as an absurdity and consoles Gregh's "nervosité délicate" by delicate counsel: "Ne t'agite pas d'une chose idiote, ne t'énerve pas, je t'assure que c'est comme si cela n'était pas, et en somme si une dissonance était utile dans tout ce concert de louanges, dans ce 'murmure d'amour élevé sur tes pas,' celle-ci est en somme agréable, a de réels avantages pour toi (quel style!)." [19]

While passing as rapidly as possible in Proust's adulatory letters over such phrases as "Je vois ton âme toujours exhaussée et rendue plus translucide ne plus rien laisser perdre de ce qui flotte de divin dans la nature et dans la vie," we are frequently detained by some quite interesting bits of criticism. There are comments and advice on matters of style valuable as testimony to Proust's literary point of view. Although the letter of June 3, 1905, begins by the lofty nonsense quoted above, it ends with a thought worthy of our attention: "Sans doute ce serait méconnaître toute la perfection que ton œuvre a atteinte que de te conseiller une forme 'curieuse,' alors que tu as la simplicité des maîtres. Mais tu sais comme moi tout ce que la fusion des émotions morales aux sensations naturelles, qui est la seule grande poésie, tend toujours à donner au style de trop abstrait et comme tu es dans le vrai chemin, à la vraie source de la grande poésie, tu ne risques pas de te perdre et de te détourner, même si tu te complais et te divertis et condescends à souligner parfois d'un trait singulier une forme parfaite. . . ." [20]

Curious recommendation, for it seems to run counter to Proust's habitual advocacy of spontaneity and his high concept of art. Of course Proust never repudiated craftsmanship, for he felt that great skill was required to record the inner vision, which is the primary material of art. Here, however, he seems to be advising his friend, with complacent

[17] Gregh, *L'Age d'airain* (Grasset, 1951), p. 53.
[18] *Ibid.,* pp. 55 ff.
[19] *Ibid.,* p. 58.
[20] Pierre-Quint, *Marcel Proust,* p. 430.

cynicism, to strive after effects, the "enjolivements" he tells Robert Dreyfus not to confuse with real style.[21] Compare this advice to Gregh with the compliment he paid Dreyfus about the same time: " Mais comme tu t'abstiens avec soin—et avec raison—. . . de beautés ajoutées et ne cherches (et trouves) la beauté que dans la pureté absolue de ta clarté qui devient précieuse quand elle éclaire des profondeurs, je me suis permis cette indication.[22] And the warning he would give Paul Morand years later in the preface to *Tendres Stocks*: "Le seul reproche que je serais tenté d'adresser à Morand, c'est qu'il a quelquefois des images autres que des images inévitables." [23]

Léon Blum

Léon Blum was fresh from the École Normale when he joined the *Banquet* staff. One may read in its pages the agreeable quatrains that the future socialist statesman dedicated to the moon and a *Méditation sur le suicide d'un de mes amis*, a Barrèsian piece which the eighteen-year-old Proust declared execrable. In publishing the letter in which Proust scores Blum's article, Fernand Gregh suggests that some literary rivalry or personal quarrel between the two young authors might explain Proust's angry tone.[24] At any rate Proust's hostility toward Blum does not seem to have been of long duration. Blum had perceived Proust's genius from the first. Of *Les Plaisirs et les jours* he had written: "J'attends avec beaucoup d'impatience son prochain livre. Quand on a le talent de style, toute l'aisance de pensée que recèle ce livre trop coquet et trop joli, ce sont là des dons qu'on ne peut laisser perdre." [25]

Proust did not forget Blum's encouragement, for twenty years afterward Proust thought of Blum as a likely person to do the article for *Figaro* on *À La Recherche du temps perdu*.

Robert de Flers and Gaston Caillavet

As a gentleman of society, Proust went frequently to the theater and counted among his friends some of the leading dramatic authors of the time: Hervieu, Porto-Riche, Bataille, Rostand, Capus, Flers and Caillavet. His precocious infatuation with the theater is recorded in some of the most memorable passages in the early volumes of *À La Recherche du temps perdu*. In love with the stage before he had seen a play, Marcel

[21] Dreyfus, p. 292.
[22] *Ibid.*, pp. 212-13.
[23] Morand, *Tendres Stocks* (Gallimard, 1923), p. 35.
[24] Gregh, " Mon Amitié avec Marcel Proust. Lettres inédites I," *La Revue des Deux Mondes*, January 1, 1954, pp. 30-32.
[25] Pierre-Quint, *Marcel Proust*, p. 42.

wove enchanting dreams about Phèdre and her great interpreter Berma. But the prewar period, with its "psychological" plays, its Realism, and its bedroom farces, does not represent a high peak in the history of the French theater. Proust recognized, and perhaps shared, the disdain generally felt for the plays of his contemporaries. This did not alter his high regard for theatrical art as such:

> Je ne discute pas le bien ou mal fondé des dédains que beaucoup de littérateurs professent aujourd'hui pour l'art du théâtre, dédains que Goethe—le plus grand auteur dramatique du XIXe siècle . . .—et Dickens ne partageaient pas. Mais enfin, il reste que tout de même c'est encore au théâtre que l'illusion de la vie est la plus parfaite. Un roman a beau être émouvant, on ne pleure jamais en le lisant comme on pleurerait au théâtre. J'ai la plus vive admiration pour les romans si originaux de Tristan Bernard. Je ne ris pas autant en les lisant qu'en écoutant quelqu'un de ces chefs-d'œuvre en un acte où il a su mettre tout son délicieux esprit.[26]

One is inclined to accept Proust's words here as a statement of his feelings, although they were written as a sort of pastiche for Antoine Bibesco. The illusion of life he speaks of here does not mean Realism, to which Proust was categorically opposed. He snapped irritably at a dramatic critic of the *N.R.F.* who praised Maurice Donnay's realistic dialogue: "J'apprends, en lisant la chronique de l'éminent écrivain auquel Jacques a confié la critique dramatique, que les personnages d'*Amants* parlent un langage moins éloigné de la réalité que ceux de Porto-Riche. Ce raisonnement met, si on le suit jusqu'au bout, les pièces de Claudel au-dessous de tout. Mais surtout, alors, rien n'est moins naturel que *Phèdre* qui me semblait fourmiller de vérité. Enfin Jarry lui-même semble un assez grand déformateur du langage naturel, puisqu'au mot merde lui-même, il a cru devoir ajouter un second r."[27] Although in tone far different from the "gaulois" banter we observe here, the passages in *Le Temps retrouvé* where Proust sets forth his esthetic ideal lampoon just as vigorously the pretensions of Realism.

Of all the men of the theater whom Proust knew, he was on closest terms with Flers and Caillavet, the writing team that for a full quarter century stood foremost in the social comedy in France. The beginnings of Proust's close friendship with Flers are announced in a letter to Robert de Billy which the recipient says he received in 1893 while on duty in Berlin. Here is the ebullient message: "Il n'y a rien d'extrêmement changé dans ma vie sentimentale, sinon que j'ai trouvé un ami, j'entends quelqu'un qui est pour moi comme j'eusse été pour X. . ., par exemple, s'il n'avait été si sec. C'est le jeune et charmant, et intelligent, et bon, et

[26] *Lettres de Marcel Proust à Bibesco* (Lausanne: Guilde du Livre, 1949), p. 162.
[27] *Lettres à la N. R. F.*, p. 187.

tendre Robert de Flers." [28] Proust and Flers had, of course, known each other for some years before, since they were lycéens together. Indeed, if we can trust Proust's memory, they had been more than casual acquaintances, close enough for Flers to feel injured when he thought that Marcel was fond of someone else. Years later, reminiscing with the recently widowed Mme Gaston de Caillavet about those days, Proust recalled Flers's jealousy of his friendship for her future husband, whom he had just met: "Mon amitié pour Gaston était immense, je ne parlais que de lui à la caserne. . . . A cette époque Robert de Flers ne connaissait pas encore Gaston qui prit même assez mal mon affection pour son futur collaborateur." [29] Proust had encountered Caillavet while calling on his mother just before going into the army. Gaston was just about through with his own service: "Il allait finir quand moi j'allais commencer et c'est au cours de brèves 'permissions' que je l'entrevis chez sa mère. Mais il y fut si délicieux pour moi que notre amitié commença tout de suite." [30] While Marcel was away at Orléans, the two friends wrote to each other during the week, and when Marcel had a week-end pass, it was Gaston who took him to the station on Sunday evening to board the train back to Orléans. Eventually Proust, Caillavet, and Flers, all three, joined hands in affectionate comradeship.

Mme de Caillavet's drawing room became the headquarters from which the trio made frequent excursions in society. They often could be seen together at Madeleine Lemaire's, where Reynaldo Hahn performed his own compositions. Perhaps of the two, Proust saw somewhat more of Flers. In 1893 Proust and Flers were seeing each other almost daily. They worked together on the *Banquet*, and Proust obtained permission from Montesquiou, not always gracious toward Proust's friends, to present to him Robert de Flers. Proust never tired of Flers's company. In 1904 he could still write to him: "Tu es un ami exquis que j'adore." [31] His feelings toward Caillavet were no less affectionate. Writing his letter of condolence to Caillavet's widow, he cried, "J'adorais Gaston, ma tendresse pour lui était infinie." [32]

As Proust declined in health he was forced to see less and less of his friends. But he followed with greatest interest their theatrical ventures together and mustered his force to attend their plays: "Je ne sais comment j'ai eu la force d'aller au *Roi*. Mais cela a été pour moi un merveilleux enchantement." [33] "Ce merveilleux Vergy [*Le Sire de Vergy*,

[28] Robert de Billy, *Marcel Proust* (Ed. des Portiques, 1930), p. 103.
[29] *Correspondance générale*, IV, 138.
[30] *Ibid.*, p. 137.
[31] *Ibid.*, p. 97.
[32] *Ibid.*, pp. 130-31.
[33] *Ibid.*, p. 98.

de Robert de Flers et G.-A. Caillavet] qui est une des plus délicieuses choses que j'ai vues, et où j'applaudissais si fort que j'ai failli trois fois donner des claques à mon voisin, M. Hervieu." [34]

From 1913 on, Proust called frequently upon the services of Flers, who had gained prominence in literature and the theater. He entrusted to him the publicity for *Swann.* Flers, in his capacity of co-director with Alfred Capus of *Figaro,* put himself generously at Proust's disposition, offering publicity and reviews.

Louis de Robert

When Proust published his translation of Ruskin, Louis de Robert, whose career was then at its height, was among the few to notice the event and write Proust of his sincere admiration. Robert had recognized also the talent displayed in *Les Plaisirs et les jours* and predicted for its author a brilliant future. He could claim, moreover, to be the "premier ami" of Swann: "Peu de temps avant sa mort, je reçus de Marcel Proust les trois tomes de *Sodome et Gomorrhe* II avec une dédicace où se lisait cette phrase: 'La dernière pensée du malade sera pour le premier ami de Swann.'" [35] Proust had much to thank Robert for in encouraging and fostering his literary career. He repaid his benefactor by a keen interest and a generous esteem for his writings.

The friendship between Louis de Robert and Proust sprang up during the Dreyfus Affair, which would be for a long time its strongest bond. They had been introduced to each other by Edmond Sée through a chance encounter on the boulevard Malesherbes. Proust introduced Robert to Mme de Caillavet, who asked him to dinner. But even the proximity of Anatole France did not compensate for the discomfort Robert felt in society. His poverty made him diffident about accepting invitations and even made him feel that financial and social differences between his situation and Proust's would stand in the way of their friendship. Eventually, however, Proust succeeded in overcoming Robert's misgivings and scruples to the point of making him accept valuable gifts. In the days of the Dreyfus Affair they would often meet at Weber's in the rue Royale. Weber's, at the turn of the century, was a favorite haunt of men of letters and artists. Léon Daudet has described Proust as he arrived there: "Vers 7h. 1/2 arrivait chez Weber un jeune homme pâle, aux yeux de biche, suçant ou tripotant une moitié de sa moustache brune et tombante, entouré de lainage comme un bibelot chinois. Il demandait une grappe de raisin, un verre d'eau et déclarait qu'il venait de se lever, qu'il avait la grippe, qu'il s'allait recoucher, que le bruit lui faisait mal,

[34] *Ibid.,* pp. 114-15.

[35] Robert, *Comment Débuta Marcel Proust* (Gallimard, 1926), p. 11.

jetait autour de lui des regards inquiets, puis moqueurs, en fin de compte éclatait d'un rire enchanté et restait." [36]

Their really deep friendship began, however, with Robert's novel, *Le Roman d'un malade*. Delicate health created strong sympathy between the two men, and Proust was deeply impressed by this account of an invalid whose days are numbered. In giving artistic form to the tragedy of his life, Robert spoke for all invalids in language so touching as to move a person in perfect health. Its effect upon a fellow sufferer would be powerful indeed. Proust must have pondered long over the last lines of the novel. They formulate precisely his own great ambition to finish his work before death should overtake him:

> Je sais qu'on peut trouver absurde le beau rêve orgueilleux de se survivre, et pourtant j'avoue qu'il m'eût été doux de fermer les yeux avec la sensation de laisser une trace dans la mémoire de ceux, tous ceux qui auront pu me comprendre, à qui j'ai essayé de montrer ici un peu de mon cœur. Mourir quand on est assuré de laisser derrière soi un souvenir un peu durable de son passage; quand de votre voix qui s'est tue demeurent tant d'échos qu'ils font ressaillir le passant à tous les coins du chemin; quand, à chaque instant de l'avenir, des amoureux et des poètes doivent murmurer votre nom avec plus de ferveur que celui de leur maîtresse; quand on peut prévoir qu'un jour un vieillard, en se découvrant, dira, dans un religieux silence, à des jeunes hommes émus: "Voilà le banc où il s'est assis," mourir dans ces conditions, ce n'est pas retourner au néant, c'est s'endormir.[37]

For Proust, literature was the goal and the highest good in life.

After Proust had completed his own work and was ready to give *Swann* to the public, he turned naturally to Robert as a friend and successful author with professional experience and connections. Robert advised him against publishing his work at his own expense, for fear of the stigma of amateur that such a step might entail. He wrote to Ollendorff, recommending Proust's book to the firm. His letter prompted the reply from Humblot which has become famous: "Cher ami, je suis peut-être bouché à l'émeri, mais je ne puis comprendre qu'un monsieur puisse employer trente pages à décrire comment il se tourne et se retourne dans son lit avant de trouver le sommeil." [38] After Grasset had accepted the work, Proust continued to call upon Robert concerning last-minute details. It was through the latter's persuasion that Proust abandoned the bulky format he had first insisted upon, agreeing to put in chapter indentations and limit the first volume to 500 pages. They discussed at length the matter of the title, but in the end Proust decided in favor of his original idea: *Du Côté de chez Swann*. When the book appeared, Robert under-

[36] Léon Daudet, *Salons et journaux* (Nouvelle Librairie Nationale, 1917), p. 298.
[37] Robert, *Le Roman d'un malade* (Fasquelle, 1911), concluding passage.
[38] Robert, *Comment Débuta Marcel Proust*, p. 13.

took to obtain for it the Goncourt award. Here again Robert's efforts were not repaid by success. Proust, however, was deeply grateful for Robert's constant encouragement and willingness to help, and his last thoughts were for the "premier ami" of Swann.

Jacques-Emile Blanche

Ceux qui étudient la vie littéraire ou artistique de la France ou de l'Angleterre au cours des vingt-cinq ans qui précédèrent la première guerre mondiale rencontrent fréquemment le nom du peintre Jacques-Emile Blanche.[39]

The portrait of Marcel Proust at the age of twenty was painted by Jacques-Emile Blanche. He is doubtless best known as a painter, although his gifts as a writer have caused people to regret that he did not devote more time to literature. As an art critic he has been ranked with Delacroix and Fromentin. Besides his essays and criticism, he is the author of a number of novels and novelettes, among which *Aymeris* is best remembered. Blanche was one of Proust's lifelong friends; we can reconstruct something of their long association by means of Proust's letters and Blanche's reminiscences.[40]

As a boy Blanche lived in Auteuil not far from Proust's maternal relatives, the Weils, in whose garden Proust used to spend a good part of his summer vacations. He was ten years older than Proust, however, and apparently did not meet him until Proust's military service in 1889. With the amused condescension that colors all his reminiscences of Proust (due perhaps to his ten years' seniority), Blanche observed the young dandy making his debut in society, courting dowagers and hobnobbing with the young gentlemen whom Proust referred to as "les jeunes ducs."[41] This is the time of the well-known portrait. Would that we had others that Blanche could have left us of Proust! There is a word sketch of him in uniform: "Je le revois en capote militaire déboutonnée, shako de lignard. Quelle étrange combinaison faisaient sa chevelure, le pur ovale de sa face de jeune Assyrien, avec l'uniforme de soldat qui n'était certes pas de fantaisie."[42] But the only other canvas he did of Proust did not please him and was destroyed. Proust declined an invitation to sit again. And the family would not permit Blanche to do a portrait from the death mask.

Fresh from the lycée, Proust and his comrades held Blanche in respect and deference for his associations with the Symbolists and the Impres-

[39] Jean Simon, "Jacques-Emile Blanche et l'Angleterre," *Revue de Littérature Comparée*, April-June, 1952, p. 183.

[40] "Lettres à Jacques-Emile Blanche," *Correspondance générale*, III, 103-75; Blanche, *Mes Modèles*.

[41] *Ibid.*, p. 100. [42] *Ibid.*, p. 108.

sionists, with their idols like Barrès. But Proust's warm feelings for Blanche could not develop as he might have wished. Blanche was far less impressed than Proust by the delights of associating with the *gratin,* and refused to follow him into the salons where both were invited. As Proust moved into the Montesquiou orbit he had to forgo the pleasure of the company of his "portraitist," as he pretentiously referred to Blanche in a letter to the count.[43] Montesquiou disliked Blanche, and although Proust protested at the injustice to his friend, he bowed before Montesquiou's veto. Blanche describes these years as "des années de méfiance à mon égard, d'obéissance au veto de Robert de Montesquiou."[44] A factor that heightened the tension between the two was the Dreyfus case. Blanche found Proust "passionné, buté, doctrinaire."[45] And Proust, even twenty years after the Affair, reproached Blanche for not having taken a firmer stand: ". . . pourquoi n'avoir pas pris position nette dans l'Affaire? . . . Ne protestez pas, cher ami, *vous étiez tiède, peu sûr.* . . . On vous surveillait. Il fallait qu'on se comptât! Vous auriez dû être avec nous."[46]

Beginning with the war years Blanche and Proust came close together again. They exchanged frequent visits and wrote to one another at length. Proust read proof for his friend and offered generous advice on points of style and grammar. Blanche's invitation to Proust to do the preface to his book on painters[47] gave rise to one of those bewildering entanglements that Proust so frequently got into. Blanche, for his part, was not by any means a simple and forthright person, if we are to believe what Léon Daudet says about him: "Il appartient à la race des commères tragiques, brouillant les gens sous prétexte de les réconcilier, compliquant les histoires les plus simples. . . ."[48] In consenting to do the preface (because friendship forbade him refuse),[49] Proust begged Blanche not to advertise the fact because he had refused so many others. Apparently Blanche did not keep the secret very well, for Proust reproached him sharply. In the midst of the writing Proust suspected—and rightly so—that Blanche had misgivings regarding the preface he would produce. Their difficulties became so involved that, as we read Proust's letters, we wonder how the work was ever turned out. But their mutual esteem finally triumphed, and their last communications seem very friendly. Blanche

[43] *Correspondance générale,* I, 100.
[44] *Mes Modèles,* p. 125.
[45] *Ibid.,* p. 135.
[46] *Ibid.,* p. 114.
[47] Blanche, *Propos de peintre* (Emile-Paul, 1919).
[48] *Salons et journaux,* pp. 226-27.
[49] "Mais Blanche a fait autrefois mon portrait, c'est un vieil ami, le livre m'est dédié, il m'était difficile de le lui refuser." *Correspondance générale,* III, 4.

recalls the pleasure of their last encounter: "Cette dernière visite ne fut que rires, un enchantement; toute notre jeunesse évoquée au chevet de l'artiste et de l'ami pour qui j'avais le plus de considération, il me faut dire: de passion." [50]

One of the letters to Blanche contains the discussion frequently referred to of the relative value of first versions and finished products. Proust would like to quote in his preface to *Propos de peintre* passages from an earlier version of the work. To justify his preference for the uncorrected text, he declares as follows:

> En principe, je trouve, et par raison de doctrine, absurde, de préférer une première version, une esquisse, etc. Sainte-Beuve prétendait toujours "ne pas retrouver dans les éditions suivantes, la flamme, etc." C'est vraiment trop nier le travail organique selon lequel un atome se développe et se fructifie. Je trouverais donc idiot de déclarer vos secondes versions inférieures. Je me ferais l'effet des gens qui aiment dans Molière, non *le Misanthrope* mais *l'Etourdi,* dans Musset, non *les Nuits* mais *la Ballade à la Lune,* c'est-à-dire tout ce que Molière et Musset ont tâché d'abandonner pour des formes plus hautes. Malgré cela et le principe proclamé, il peut se faire . . . qu'un premier jet ait une sève, que des corrections trop restrictives arrêteront. . . .[51]

He suggests it might be interesting for the public to have two versions so as to compare the version of his quotations with the final one of the text. Not that he approves Claudel's custom of publishing three "states" of the same drama ("ce que je trouve insensé"). A poet must be able to choose and sacrifice, but a prefacer may be justified in offering a document.

The passage poses a problem of interpretation. Proust's remarks may, of course, be motivated by other than esthetic considerations. He may merely not wish to give himself the additional trouble of correcting the passages he has already utilized and having to modify his comments; he may be using this roundabout way of disapproving Blanche's corrected version. But if we take the words at their face value, we see Proust on the horns of the esthetic dilemma: inspiration or craftsmanship, which is more important? He recognizes that a spontaneous work may be superior to one fashioned with great care. But by his reservations we are apt to see in Proust little more than a timid precursor of the partisans of pure spontaneity. His avowal is made with something like indignation or resentment, and the statement "J'ai tellement pris l'habitude de distinguer chez un écrivain 'le fond et la forme'" shows that the conventional dichotomy was basic in his esthetic thinking.

[50] *Hommage à Marcel Proust* (Gallimard, 1927), p. 54.
[51] *Correspondance générale,* III, 139.

Jean-Louis Vaudoyer

Jean-Louis Vaudoyer, poet, novelist, and art critic, is typical of the men of letters with whom Proust surrounded himself. For the most part they are writers whose names are still known, but who are little read. The books of Vaudoyer, like those of Robert, receive only brief mention in literary manuals today. In spite of talent and culture, these authors lack the great significance necessary to make literary history. But they do make pleasant reading still, and we are happy for an opportunity to further our acquaintance with writers, whom, were it not for their association with Proust, we might well have continued to neglect.

The name of Vermeer somehow spans or encompasses the friendship between Marcel Proust and Jean-Louis Vaudoyer. In his first letter to Vaudoyer, Proust spoke of Vermeer and their common admiration for him. Years later they went to the Tuileries together to view the "petit pan de mur si bien peint en jaune." Proust was very ill, and paid for the pleasure he took in the exposition by a severe attack. His sufferings at the time were carefully noted to serve later to describe Bergotte's death.

Proust and Vaudoyer had met in 1910 at a performance of the Ballets Russes. Afterward Proust wrote to compliment Vaudoyer on his *Variations sur les ballets russes*. Thus began an epistolary exchange which was to last until Proust's death. As with Robert, Proust called upon Vaudoyer for expert and technical counsel regarding his novel. He sought his opinion on matters of type, of paging, titles and divisions, and financial arrangements. The letters of 1913 on reveal an ill and harried author, unable to cope by himself with the thousand practical matters involved in writing and publishing.

More interesting to us, however, are the letters in which Proust speaks of Vaudoyer's writing. He was first charmed by Vaudoyer's verse: "J'ai beaucoup pensé à vous, beaucoup vécu avec vos vers délicieux, avec eux, par eux, à travers eux, en eux, grâce à eux. . . ."[52] Novels such as *La Maîtresse et l'amie* are hailed just as enthusiastically. Let us look at one of Proust's letters praising a new work. It is typical of his technique which, although often carried to the point of ridiculousness, shows a rare virtuosity. That is to say, whereas the hyperbolic tone may invalidate his critical remarks as an honest appraisal, they remain a fine piece of writing for their delicate analysis and exquisite phrasing. Precious invention and sensitivity combine to give them a particular beauty long out of fashion. Observe him thanking Vaudoyer for a volume of his poems (*Poésies*, Calmann-Lévy, 1913). He declares that the verses improve with reading: "Votre art est si minutieux et si profond que l'attention la plus clair-

[52] *Ibid.*, IV, 37.

voyante n'y peut d'abord tout découvrir."[53] To express this simple thought Proust contrives a very flattering metaphor: "Selon que je vous lis, je vois de nouveaux vers restés dans l'ombre jusqu'ici s'illuminer au point qu'ils éclipsent ceux que je leur avais préférés d'abord, comme ces parcelles d'un vitrail que la mobilité d'un rayon ou seulement un mouvement que nous faisons dans la nef éteignent et rallument tour à tour." Metaphors give way to literary allusions when with iconoclastic zeal Proust pushes the great poets from their niches to enshrine his friend: "Il n'y a rien dans Leconte de Lisle au fond des mots de qui on puisse descendre plus avant qu'on ne fait dans la pièce qui ouvre le recueil, *Du trait dont le soleil a blessé le feuillage*, que j'égale aux plus purs *Poèmes antiques*; ni dans Chénier qui soit aussi souplement articulé que les vers d'*Hébé dansante*." Paradox, antithesis, and other rhetorical devices are deployed in honor of the subject: "Votre délicieuse *Suzanne et l'Italie* prend de tous ces voisinages une force singulière, car plus vous êtes largement objectif et plus vous êtes vous-même et ce qui émerveille dans ces poésies c'est autant l'étendue de leur rayonnement que le centre permanent de leur convergence." Today, when nobody reads Vaudoyer's poetry anyway, it matters little whether these remarks of Proust have great validity. Their value is now almost wholly esthetic, an example of an alembicated and bejeweled art at which Proust is one of the great masters.

Incidental to the volumes upon which he is commenting, Proust has much of general interest to say. One thinks of the ingenious justification he offers for the pleasure serious readers can take in de luxe bindings: "C'est la seule forme sous laquelle je puisse aimer et posséder de jolies choses, comme prolongement à une œuvre d'art, et excitant d'ailleurs à de nouveaux rêves qui nourrissent à leur tour la lecture qu'on a faite. Ce sont des couvertures, des enveloppes; on va du livre à elles, mais on retourne d'elles au livre. Ce cercle ininterrompu est enchanteur, enchanté."[54]

Although Proust claimed to admire everything Vaudoyer wrote, he disagrees with him frequently in his literary views and tastes. Vaudoyer devoted much study to Théophile Gautier and held him in great esteem. Proust accepts Vaudoyer's eulogistic comments on the author of *Emaux et camées* with serious reservation. *Le Capitaine Fracasse* is, incidentally, the work of Gautier that Proust preferred. In commenting upon Vaudoyer's study, he is led to observations regarding the value of personal or anecdotal information about an artist that would furnish ammunition to the "New Critics" and all the anti-biographers of today: "D'autre

[53] *Ibid.*, p. 59.
[54] *Ibid.*, p. 38.

part, je comprends que la figure parisienne et boulevardière de Cocteau . . . n'ajoute aucun intérêt à *la Danse de Sophocle.* Mais est-il beaucoup plus important d'apprendre qu'un M. Léautaud . . . se fait faire des pardessus sans poches et tire des crins de sa doublure? J'avoue que l'intérêt pris par l'Eckermann de la *Revue française* à ces particularités de quelqu'un qui n'a écrit ni *les Affinités électives* ni *les Années d'apprentissage,* me paraît fantastique. . . ." [55]

The last letter, like the first written twelve years before, speaks of one artist about whom they had no difference of opinion—Vermeer. Proust sealed his friendship with these words written on a copy of *Sodome et Gomorrhe* II: "Je garde le souvenir lumineux du seul matin que j'aie revu et où vous avez guidé affectueusement mes pas qui chancelaient trop vers ce Ver Meer où les pignons des maisons 'sont comme de précieux objets chinois.'" [56]

René Boylesve

René Boylesve once declared bitterly that Proust had accomplished what he himself had always dreamed of. And it is quite true that in his first books particularly he seems to have paved the way for Proust. There are stylistic similarities and a common dedication to the analysis of love. As a young writer, Boylesve exercised little constraint upon his pen, permitting himself a verbal richness and syntactical profuseness that resemble Proust's style. But in 1899 when he submitted a manuscript, "Bonnets de dentelle," to Ganderax, the director of the *Revue de Paris,* he was taken seriously to task for his prolixity. Boylesve accepted his chastisement without a murmur and rewrote the work, which we know under the title *La Becquée.* This established Boylesve's definitive stylistic technique. Ganderax's counsel, his own classical training, and his admiration for Flaubert, all contributed to make him feel that the sacrifice of his natural expression was worth while.

One knows how well Boylesve adapted himself to his new discipline. He became a master of the sober and elegant art that distinguishes the period and places him close to his great contemporaries Anatole France and Henri de Régnier. His delicate painting of bourgeois life and his psychological analysis, free from *parti pris* or ulterior message, are in an authentic French tradition. He permitted himself only, like France and Régnier, the coloration of a very urbane irony.

The impact of Proust's work upon a writer who had submitted to such rigid discipline could be no less than terrific. In Proust, Boylesve could see the triumph of a style he had ruthlessly suppressed twenty-five years

[55] *Ibid.,* p. 53.
[56] *Ibid.,* p. 90.

before. His first reactions were naturally hostile. But, upon reading the successive volumes of *À La Recherche du temps perdu* that appeared after the war, Boylesve's honesty and admiration prevailed over his prejudices. With sad resignation he announced to his friends: "Notre œuvre à nous est ruinée par celle-là. Nous avons travaillé en vain. Proust supprime la littérature des cinquante dernières années." [57] He might have reread with wry amusement a compliment Proust once addressed to him: "Or les 'clichés' que *le Bonheur à cinq sous* fait prendre à Souzouches, c'est la miniature achevée, où tout est dit. Ah! combien souvent faisant un mélancolique retour sur moi quand je vous lis je m'applique ce vers de Molière:

> Boylesve avec deux mots en eût dit plus que vous." [58]

Proust's admiration for Boylesve was quite genuine: "Vos livres sont pour moi, comme des lettres d'amour: on les range, puis on les classe autrement, on ne perd aucune occasion de les relire, on les a toujours auprès de soi." [59] He preferred Boylesve's early works. Even at a time when his esteem for Boylesve faltered a bit, he remembered with pleasure his impression of the early works: "Je ne sais si c'est moi qui ai changé ou lui mais il me semblait qu'au temps de *La Becquée* et de *L'Enfant à la Balustrade,* c'etait ravissant tout le temps." [60] When Martin-Chauffier sneered at Jacques Boulenger for praising Boylesve in *Mais L'Art est difficile!* Proust's indignation was aroused. He wrote Boulenger: "Et aux livres délicieux et préférés de vous que vous citez, moi, il me semble que j'ajouterais *la Becquée, l'Enfant à la Balustrade,* que je trouve supérieurs, et même *le Médecin des Dames de Néans.*" [61] Practically from his deathbed he wrote their author: "Je ne serai jamais infidèle au *Médecin des Dames de Néans,* à *la Becquée,* à l'*Enfant à la Balustrade. . . .*" [62] The last two works, although at the time generally considered inferior to the love novels, Proust described as the "fine flower" of Boylesve's genius. Of all Boylesve's novels, they have best stood the test of time, and today academic and critical opinion concurs with Proust's taste.

In these novels, written at the turn of the century, Boylesve paints with infinite exactitude the life of old provincial towns. He knew the life well, having been born in a village in Touraine and growing up, like little Riquet Nadaud, in the very atmosphere he describes in *La Becquée* and *L'Enfant à la balustrade.* In subject and treatment these provincial scenes

[57] Cited by A. Bourgeois, *René Boylesve* (Droz, 1945), p. 24.
[58] *Correspondance générale,* IV, 152-53.
[59] *Ibid.,* p. 157.
[60] *À Un Ami,* p. 219.
[61] *Correspondance générale,* III, 249.
[62] *Ibid.,* IV, 157.

anticipate parts of *Swann* in which Proust describes Combray. It is not too much to assume that Proust could owe something to Boylesve in the first part of Chapter II, where he graphically presents the country town, with its streets and its square. Tante Léonie and Françoise have much in common with the provincial types encountered in Boylesve's novels.

Proust's acknowledgment of a complimentary copy of *Le Bonheur à cinq sous* gives us the opportunity of looking at these stories through his eyes. The one whose title is given to the entire volume elicits high enthusiasm. It is indeed a delightful piece. Jérôme Jeton is an aspiring *homme de lettres,* held to his goal by his ambitious wife, who feels that being "somebody" is worth sacrificing all natural inclination and enduring an existence neither comfortable nor basically satisfying. Jérôme has no illusions regarding his talents, writes without love, and esteems his wretched pieces at their just value. Through his wife's social efforts he is commissioned to do a novel, a task far beyond his capacities. At the same time he is offered a country house for the summer, and the two set forth at once. Salving their consciences with the thought that the novel can be written here as well as in Paris, they abandon themselves to the joys of country living, what their temperaments have fitted them for all along. The novel, of course, does not get written, and they are on the point of admitting that they should give in to their inclination and remain happily in the country when they are suddenly invaded by reporters come to photograph the author in his rural retreat. Phrases like "cher maître," "grand mission" rain about them. There is no more question of the simple life. They return to Paris.

Je ne crois pas que vous ayez encore opposé d'une façon aussi parfaite, aussi concentrée dans sa composition symétrique, le bonheur . . . d'une vie passée dans un *Bout du Point* et la mesquinerie factice de la fausse vie de salon. Naturellement, à cette vie factice, personne avant vous ne s'était avisé de lui donner un corps. . . . Je sais que vous avez écrit de plus grands livres; mais parce que j'admire l'immense fresque des *Illusions perdues* et *Splendeur et Misère,* cela ne m'empêche pas de placer au moins aussi haut *le Curé de Tours,* ou *la Vieille Fille,* ou *la Fille aux yeux d'or,* et d'égaler l'art de ces miniatures à la fresque.[63]

Proust, although no country residence could ever have lured him away from the drawing rooms of Paris, enthusiastically endorsed Boylesve's exposure of life in the capital. No one, he exclaimed, has ever thought of depicting this unnatural existence! No one, we might remark, so much as Proust himself, whose own work on the subject is the vast fresco in comparison with Boylesve's miniature.

Ah! Le Beau Chien, the story of a mutt that became a lap dog, deserves

[63] *Ibid.,* p. 152.

to be singled out for praise: "J'ai trouvé *Ah! le beau chien!* une merveille; et Spinoza l'aurait trouvé aussi d'accord pour une fois avec Labiche."[64] *Amélie ou une humeur de guerre* illustrates the martyrdom some ladies suffer at the hands of their cooks. Amélie's concern for her uncle and aunt, whose village has been bombed, moves her mistress to send for them. To the good lady's sorrow, she learns that one good deed leads to another, but each is just a new pretext for grumbling on the part of the cross-grained Amélie. Proust read it to his *femme de chambre* for its edifying effect. His lesson missed its mark, however. The servant thoroughly enjoyed the portrait and found it quite like the *femme de chambre* on the next floor, as well as the one on the floor below. Only on Proust's floor, no one resembling Amélie!

In view of Proust's constant courtesy toward Boylesve, it is painful to remember the pen portrait he has left us of Proust, which for cruel caricature exceeds Proust's own painting of grotesques.

30 septembre 1920.

Chez Mme G. B., réunion du jury pour attribuer les bourses.

J'ai vu entrer, alors que nos étions en séances depuis une demi-heure, Marcel Proust. De loin, pendant que, précédé d'un domestique en livrée, il avançait dans le corridor, j'ai cru voir, en fantôme, une interprétation humaine du *Corbeau*, d'Edgar Poë.

Un être assez grand, presque gros, les épaules hautes, engoncé dans un long pardessus. Il garde son pardessus, en malade qui craint une température fâcheuse. Mais surtout, une face extraordinaire; une chair de gibier faisandé, bleue, de larges yeux d'almée, creux, soutenus par deux épais croissants d'ombre, des cheveux abondants, droits, noirs, mal coupés et non coupés depuis deux mois, une moustache négligée, noire. Il a l'aspect d'une chiromancienne et son sourire. Quand je lui serre la main, je suis absorbé par son faux-col évasé, élimé, et qui, sans exagérer, n'a pas été changé depuis huit jours. Tenue de pauvre, avec de petits souliers fins chaussant un pied de femme. Une cravate râpée, un pantalon large, d'il y a dix ans. Je pense à tout ce qui, en sa littérature nouvellement sortie, date. Il est assis à côté de moi: je le regarde. Il a, malgré la moustache, l'air d'une dame juive de soixante ans, qui aurait été belle. Ses yeux, de profil, sont orientaux. Je cherche à voir ses mains, mais elles sont emprisonnées dans des gants blancs, remarquablement sales; en revanche je remarque un poignet fin, blanc et gras. La figure semble avoir été fondue, puis regonflée incomplètement et dérisoirement; les épaisseurs se portent au hasard et non où on les attendait. Jeune, vieux, malade et femme,—étrange personne.[65]

Did Boylesve know that the great invalid had left his bed only by the aid of drugs, and for the sole purpose of supporting a needy and worthy candidate, Jacques Rivière?

[64] *Ibid.*, p. 153.

[65] Boylesve, *Feuilles tombées* (Dumas, 1947), p. 266.

CHAPTER THREE

Other Literary Notables

Maurice Maeterlinck

Marcel Proust was a schoolboy when he first heard of Maeterlinck, whose maiden efforts were being applauded in Symbolist quarters. Proust and his chums became enthusiastic admirers of the poet of Ghent. For some years everything that Proust wrote would bear his touch. It may be felt in the *fin de siècle* style of the pieces he offered the *Banquet* and in stories such as *Violante ou la mondanité*, where the atmosphere is as unreal and dreamlike as that of *Pelléas*. He embellished his Ruskin with quotations from *La Vie des abeilles* and *La Sagesse et la destinée*.

Proust had always hoped to publish something on Maeterlinck. To Barrès he wrote: "Et dès qu'un journal me prendra des articles, si ce jour doit jamais venir, je ferai un article que j'appellerai 'qu'une vie est belle qui commence par l'art et qui finit par la morale' et qui sera sur Maeterlinck."[1] The letter refers to a discussion the two had had on Maeterlinck. What interested Proust at the moment was the two distinct parts he saw in Maeterlinck's life. He found other artists whose life seemed so divided: Racine's, Pascal's, and Tolstoi's. Barrès had assumed Proust was putting Maeterlinck on the same plane generally with Racine. Proust protests that although he meant nothing of the sort—"Je n'ai jamais prétendu les mettre sur le même plan"—he nevertheless respects Maeterlinck as a thinker: "J'ajoute que si j'avais un article à faire sur Maeterlinck, je le comparerais aussi à Virgile. Et au point de vue du talent (auquel je n'avais jamais pensé) sans doute je ne trouve pas qu'il ressemble du tout à Racine. Mais je le trouve tout de même un très grand penseur, et je le lis plus souvent." We shall notice that Proust's opinion of Maeterlinck as a thinker will at one point be less favorable and come more in line with the reservations we hold generally today. With this exception, however, Proust's high esteem and fondness for Maeterlinck continued strong throughout his life. "Vous ai-je dit le trouble—charmant —que *Pelléas* écouté—et réécouté bien des fois—au théatrophone que j'ai près de mon lit, a apporté dans mon existence?"[2] He constructed a

[1] Gramont, "Quelques Lettres inédites de Marcel Proust à Maurice Barrès," p. 99.
[2] Robert de Billy, *Marcel Proust*, p. 72.

pastiche on Maeterlinck, but it, like the one on Chateaubriand, has never appeared. Perhaps, like the Sainte-Beuve article and the novel *Jean Santeuil,* this piece too will one day be recovered.

Among the gardens Proust dreamed of writing on some day, he did not forget the garden of Maurice Maeterlinck. We can measure his admiration for the Belgian poet by the rhapsody of his phrases:

Le jardin de Maurice Maeterlinck, dominé par les images "innocentes, invariables et fraîches" d'un cyprès et d'un pin parasol, tels dit-il, dans une des plus belles pages de la prose française depuis soixante ans, qu'il "n'imagine pas de paradis ou de vie d'outre-tombe, si splendide soit-elle, où ces arbres ne soient pas à leur place." Ce jardin où le Virgile des Flandres, près des ruches de paille peintes en rose, en jaune et en bleu tendre, qui, dès l'entrée, nous rappellent ses études préférées, a recueilli tant d'incomparable poésie, peut-on bien dire qu'il n'y cherche pas autre chose que la poésie? Que,—même sans avoir besoin de descendre, à l'instar des abeilles, jusqu'aux tilleuls en fleurs ou jusqu'à l'étang où la vallisnère attend l'heure de l'amour pour s'épanouir à la surface,—il visite seulement ses lauriers-roses, près du puits, à côté de ses sauges violettes, ou explore un coin occulte de l'olivaie, ce sera pour étudier une espèce curieuse de labiée, une variété de chrysanthèmes ou d'orchidées, qui lui permettront de conclure des progrès de l'intelligence des fleurs ou des victoires que nous pouvons remporter sur leur inconscient, à d'autres progrès, à d'autres victoires aussi, qui ne seraient pas remportées celles-là dans le monde des fleurs mais rapprocheraient l'humanité de la vérité et du bonheur. Car pour cet évolutionniste dans l'absolu—si l'on peut dire,—science, philosophie et morale sont sur le même plan, et l'horizon de bonheur et de vérité n'est pas un mirage résultant des lois de notre optique et de la perspective intellectuelle, mais le terme d'un idéal réel, dont nous nous rapprochons effectivement.[3]

Reflections upon Maeterlinck's style lead Proust to one of his most interesting pronouncements regarding a writer's attitude toward his language. In a succession of pithy phrases, built upon paradox and antithesis, Proust declares the writer's liberty to write as the spirit moves him, in defiance of accepted usage and copybook regulations:

Les seules personnes qui défendent la langue française . . . ce sont celles qui "l'attaquent." Cette idée qu'il y a une langue française, existant en dehors des écrivains et qu'on protège, est inouïe. Chaque écrivain est obligé de se faire sa langue, comme chaque violoniste est obligé de se faire son "son." Et entre le son de tel violoniste médiocre, et le son (pour la même note) de Thibaut, il y a un infiniment petit, qui est un monde! Je ne veux pas dire que j'aime les écrivains originaux qui écrivent mal. Je préfère—et c'est peut-être une faiblesse—ceux qui écrivent bien. Mais ils ne commencent à écrire bien qu'à condition d'être originaux, de faire eux-mêmes leur langue. La correction, la perfection du style existe, mais au delà de l'originalité, après avoir traversé les faits, non en deça. La correction en deça "émotion discrète" "bonhomie souriante" "année abominable entre toutes" cela n'existe pas. La seule manière de défendre la langue, c'est de l'attaquer, mais oui, madame Straus! Parce que son

[3] *Correspondance générale,* II, 231-32.

unité n'est faite que de contraires neutralisés, d'une immobilité apparente qui cache une vie vertigineuse et perpétuelle. Car on ne " tient," on ne fait bonne figure, auprès des écrivains d'autrefois qu'à condition d'avoir cherché à écrire tout autrement. Et quand on veut défendre la langue française, en réalité on écrit tout le contraire du français classique. Exemple: les révolutionnaires Rousseau, Hugo, Flaubert, Maeterlinck " tiennent " à côté de Bossuet. Les néo-classiques du dix-huitième et commencement du dix-neuvième siècle, et la " bon homie souriante " et l'" émotion discrète " de toutes les époques, jurent avec les maîtres.[4]

In connection with Francis Jammes we shall have occasion to return to this subject. Correctness in style is one of the literary superstitions Proust is fond of attacking.

In 1911 Maeterlinck published a series of essays in *Figaro,* collected two years later in the volume entitled *La Mort.* Death was one of Maeterlinck's constant preoccupations, as his writings attest. He could not have thought about it more than Proust, however, who lived under its constant threat. When he read what Maeterlinck had to say on the subject, he was filled with such disappointment that he was moved for the first time to speak disparagingly of one of Maeterlinck's works. He wrote his friends about it—René Blum, Barrès, and Lauris. To the latter he said:

En lisant les articles de Maeterlinck . . . j'essayais de deviner si . . . vous éprouviez aussi la petite déception qu'ils m'ont donnée. . . . D'une façon générale je trouve qu'il y a contradiction dans les termes à parler ainsi de l'Inconnaissable comme de son cabinet de toilette en disant quand il y a doute: " Il y a trois Infinis possible. Le second est presque certain, le troisième est encore probable. Le premier n'a presque aucune chance d'être le vrai." Je sais bien qu'il y a le pari de Pascal, mais enfin cet Infini *gagnant* et cet Infini *placé* me choquent étrangement. Et puis la beauté même du style, la lourdeur de sa *carrosserie* ne conviennent pas à ces explorations de l'impalpable. Je dis carrosserie parce que je crois que c'est ainsi que parlent nos amis qui ont des automobiles et que je me souviens que je me suis permis devant vous de petites irrévérences à l'endroit de Maeterlinck—ma grande admiration du reste—en parlant d'Infini 40 chevaux et de grosses voitures marque Mystère. Mais ici mon objection est plus grave et mon livre . . . vous montrera en quoi elle consiste. Non que j'y parle de ces articles. Il y avait bien longtemps que ce que j'y ai écrit sur la mort était terminé quand ils ont paru, mais vous verrez que tout mon effort a été en sens inverse pour ne pas considérer la mort comme une négation, ce qui n'a aucun sens et ce qui est contraire à tout ce qu'elle nous fait éprouver. Elle se manifeste d'une façon terriblement positive. Et toute la beauté dont Maeterlinck sait l'entourer n'est qu'une manière de nous détourner de ce que nous sentons véritablement en face d'elle.[5]

It is difficult to understand Proust's objections to Maeterlinck's manner of speaking of death. Why should a heavy beauty of style be inappropriate

[4] *Ibid.*, VI, 92-94.
[5] *À Un Ami*, pp. 220-22.

to the solemnity of death? The funeral oration has never called for discreet or muted effects. Why should a logical and systematic examination of the problem, with conjectures based upon empirical evidence, be inappropriate in an essay? Maeterlinck is surely justified in approaching the problem with the traditional implements of western philosophical inquiry. He realizes their limitations and makes no extravagant claims for them: "Nous avons non seulement à nous résigner à vivre dans l'incompréhensible, mais à nous réjouir de n'en pouvoir sortir. S'il n'y avait plus de questions insolubles ni d'énigmes impénétrables, l'infini ne serait pas infini; et c'est alors qu'il faudrait à jamais maudire le sort qui nous aurait mis dans un univers proportionné à notre intelligence." [6] It is clear from these conclusions that Maeterlinck's claims for his method are not excessive. His book is a sober, unpretentious meditation designed to give comfort to a humanity terrified at the thought of one day dying. It deserves to be better known.

Aside from style, Proust has grave objections concerning Maeterlinck's attitude toward death. Maeterlinck tries to make death, Proust feels, a negation, and camouflages its terribly positive appearance by beauty. Indeed it is true that Maeterlinck tries to console by demonstrating that although there is little hope for an immortality such as is generally yearned for, this sort of survival is not worth having, and that a greater one probably awaits us. Proust's use of the words positive and negative is troublesome here. Since he is opposing his own notion of death to that of Maeterlinck, we can establish the following contrapositives—Proust: positive-terrible; Maeterlinck: negative-beautiful. But do not the words hold for Proust a deeper metaphysical sense? We infer they do from the phrase: " tout mon effort a été en sens inverse pour ne pas considérer la mort comme une négation, ce qui n'a aucun sens et qui est contraire à tout ce qu'elle nous fait éprouver." Here he appears to be objecting to Maeterlinck's denial of personal immortality. But how is this an easy consolation for humanity? Negation of an afterlife would strike most people as far more terrible than any positive affirmation of its existence. The association of positive-terrible, negative-beautiful in a metaphysical sense seems strange, but it is perhaps unfruitful to linger over this question of words in a letter written in haste and in which impressions are presented in a jumbled and ambiguous fashion. Without further elucidation they do not contribute to our knowledge of Proust's attitude toward death. What they do reveal is the curious fact that Proust found himself at variance with Maeterlinck when actually their views coincide on some very basic points.

Proust declares that he has stated his views on death previously and

[6] Maeterlinck, *La Mort* (Pasquelle, 1913), p. 271.

apparently he has nothing more to add. He never presented them systematically as does Maeterlinck here, but the subject is in a broad sense the theme of his entire work, and his philosophy and esthetic are patently adjustments to the eventuality that all mortals face. His earliest work, *Les Plaisirs et les jours,* sounds the death knell that will continue throughout all the volumes of *Temps perdu.* Its first item, *La Mort de Baldassare Silvande,* depicts the anxiety of a child who contemplates death for the first time. Grief-stricken little Alexis, watching his uncle die, makes us think of Marcel, who will watch the death agony of his grandmother and Bergotte. The death scenes in *Temps perdu* constitute a pinnacle of Proust's art. They have been studied with great acuity by Ramon Fernandez, who, moreover, has treated the subject of Proust's attitude toward death more completely than anyone else.[7]

Faced with the loss of his loved ones and his friends, Marcel gives himself over to a grief so poignant that it is understandable how such a person could feel that Maeterlinck did not emphasize enough the shock and horror before death. They are sentiments that Proust could never escape through rationalization. But he finds thoughts more conforting than Maeterlinck's consolation that our ego is too miserable and insignificant to be worth saving as such in the hereafter.

Does Proust have any more faith in a personal resurrection than Maeterlinck? Only when Marcel is distraught at the news of Albertine's death is even the wish for a personal survival formulated. He goes no farther than the conjecture he makes at Bergotte's death:

Il était mort. Mort à jamais? Qui peut le dire? Certes, les expériences spirites, pas plus que les dogmes religieux, n'apportent la preuve que l'âme subsiste. Ce qu'on peut dire, c'est que tout se passe dans notre vie comme si nous y entrions avec le faix d'obligations contractées dans une vie antérieure; il n'y a aucune raison, dans nos conditions de vie sur cette terre, pour que nous nous croyions obligés à faire le bien, à être délicats, même à être polis, ni pour l'artiste cultivé à ce qu'il se croie obligé de recommencer vingt fois un morceau dont l'admiration qu'il excitera importera peu à son corps mangé par les vers, comme le pan de mur jaune que peignit avec tant de science et de raffinement un artiste à jamais inconnu, à peine identifié sous le nom de Ver Meer. Toutes ces obligations, qui n'ont pas leur sanction dans la vie présente, semblent appartenir à un monde différent, fondé sur la bonté, le scrupule, le sacrifice, un monde entièrement différent de celui-ci, et dont nous sortons pour naître à cette terre, avant peut-être d'y retourner revivre sous l'empire de ces lois inconnues auxquelles nous avons obéi parce que nous en portions l'enseignement en nous, sans savoir qui les y avait tracées—ces lois dont tout travail profond de l'intelligence nous rapproche et qui sont invisibles seulement—et encore!—pour les sots. De sorte que l'idée que Bergotte n'était pas mort à jamais est sans invraisemblance.[8]

[7] Fernandez, *Proust* (Ed. de la Nouvelle Revue Critique, 1943).
[8] *La Prisonnière* (Gallimard, 1923), I, 232-33.

Personal immortality and the hypothesis of a world of the hereafter are merely suggested but never actually affirmed in Proust. His metaphorical bent and general reticence keep us from taking words like hereafter, resurrection, death itself, in a very literal sense.

Integral survival of the personality in the hereafter presupposes that the personality has an unchanging core, an individual identity or uniqueness. All Proust's works demonstrate the contrary, that "notre 'moi' est fait de la superposition de nos états successifs," [9] that the individual changes from moment to moment: "Ma vie m'apparut—offrant une succession de périodes dans lesquelles, après un certain intervalle, rien de ce qui soutenait la précédente ne subsistait plus dans celle qui la suivait—comme quelque chose de si dépourvu du support d'un moi individuel, identique et permanent, quelque chose de si inutile dans l'avenir, et de si long dans le passé, que la mort pourrait aussi bien en terminer le cours ici ou là, sans nullement le conclure." [10] Maeterlinck, one might remark, conjectures that this life is just an episode in the career of a personality. He feels, like Proust here, that the individual passes through so many complete changes in this life that it is difficult to accept the notion of death as more than another in a series of transformations. How can we expect to maintain after death an identity that we are constantly in the process of losing in life? This mysterious point of identity, "nous le perdions à tout moment de la vie." [11] Proust says too: "Nous désirons passionnément qu'il y ait une autre vie où nous serions pareils à ce que nous sommes ici-bas. Mais nous ne réfléchissons pas que, même sans attendre cette autre vie, dans celle-ci, au bout de quelques années, nous sommes infidèles à ce que nous avons été, à ce que nous voulions rester immortellement." [12] Thus death is already about us. Proust asserts: "Alors notre moi serait changé . . . ce serait donc une vraie mort de nous-mêmes, mort suivie, il est vrai, de résurrection, mais en un moi différent . . . mort fragmentaire et successive telle qu'elle s'insère dans toute la durée de notre vie." [13]

Yet, in spite of the most drastic changes, the sentiment of a single unique personality persists. What constitutes the factor in personality that is constant and assures its uniqueness? Both Proust and Maeterlinck find this factor in the memory. Maeterlinck says: "En somme, le point le plus fixe de cette nébuleuse est notre mémoire." [14] Memory is for Proust the

[9] *Albertine disparue* (Gallimard, 1925), p. 158.
[10] *Ibid.*, p. 219.
[11] *La Mort,* p. 54.
[12] *Sodome et Gomorrhe* (Gallimard, 1921-24), I, 329.
[13] *À L'Ombre des jeunes filles en fleurs,* II, 89-90.
[14] *La Mort,* p. 41.

great unifying factor that prevents the personality from disintegration and dispersement in the course of time.

Recognition of the role of memory as an integrating factor in personality has, however, quite a dissimilar effect on these two authors. Maeterlinck finds it a sufficient reason to question the desirability of survival, as well as its plausibility: "Cette hypothèse, en ses stricts limites, n'est que fort peu probable et médiocrement désirable." [15] Proust, on the contrary, devotes the bulk of his work to the analysis of what Maeterlinck calls "la misérable mémoire," and makes of it the basis of his esthetic. We know that the stuff of art was for Proust the data of memory. By a play on words, he shifts between the metaphysical and the esthetic. If memory is identical with personality and art is the record of memory, then the survival of his art implies the survival of his memory, that is to say personal immortality. After Bergotte died: "On l'enterra, mais toute la nuit funèbre, aux vitrines éclairées, ses livres, disposés trois par trois veillaient comme des anges aux ailes éployées et semblaient, pour celui qui n'était plus, le symbole de sa résurrection." [16] Bergotte's immortality will depend upon the survival of his work. This sort of immortality, although a figure of speech, had for Proust more reality than the survival of his personality in another world. He hoped to conquer death by living beyond the grave in the printed page. As a great artist himself, Maeterlinck would surely not disagree. In view of the remarkable accord of the two thinkers concerning the role of memory and the concept of an inconstant ego, it is surprising that Proust should not have hailed Maeterlinck's work as one of the soundest and most lucid essays on death ever written.

With the exception of this one work, Proust's loyalty to Maeterlinck remained perfectly constant. Frequent allusions to his work indicate great familiarity. To Mme Straus, who has been ill, he writes: "Vous allez vous sentir comme un enfant de Maeterlinck avec des sensations d'une fraîcheur exquise pour toutes les choses naturelles et bonnes." [17] Time after time he defended Maeterlinck from his detractors: it is one of the proofs of Mme de Guermantes's stupidity that she does not appreciate Maeterlinck. Her mockery of *Les Sept Princesses* so much vexes Marcel that his ardor for her immediately cools. The scorn of the younger generation for Maeterlinck was likewise irritating: "Songe que je n'ai aucune situation, et peut-être est-ce mieux ainsi, car avec l'instabilité du goût actuel, en voyant les 'jeunes' traiter déjà avec tant de mépris Maeterlinck et Régnier, si jamais on doit me trouver un peu de talent, il vaut mieux que ce soit le plus tard possible." [18] When Maeterlinck was disparaged in the reviews, Proust's sarcasm waxed hot: "J'ignore quel est le Monsieur

[15] *Ibid.*, p. 258. [16] *La Prisonnière*, I, 233.
[17] *Correspondance générale*, VI, 23. [18] *Lettres à Bibesco*, p. 146.

qui, dans la *Nouvelle Revue Française, éreinte* Maeterlinck; mais cela m'a exaspéré." [19]

Although Proust permitted himself "de petites irrévérences à l'endroit de Maeterlinck," he was ready to take up his defense when others presumed to attack him.

Jules Lemaître

Jules Lemaître was another among the exciting "moderns" to whom the boys of Condorcet had vowed a cult. Something of their enthusiasm is reflected in the description the seventeen-year-old Marcel Proust wrote for their magazine, the *Revue Lilas*: "Vu Jules Lemaître pour la première fois. Jolie tête de jeune taureau, face de faune songeur avec deux yeux d'un bleu bien pur, bleus comme un reflet de pervenche dans une source claire." [20] The fledgling writers imitated the phrasings and the neologisms of the Impressionistic critic. As late as 1908 Proust felt obliged to warn Robert Dreyfus repeatedly against locutions that savored too much of Lemaître. Of course, he explained, "J'aime Lemaître, mais aucun imitateur." [21]

After his debut in society Proust was privileged to know Lemaître personally, just as he had met another literary lion, Anatole France. Lemaître took favorable notice of young Proust at the dinners and receptions where they would meet. His praise for the *Pastiches* was very gratifying to Proust: "M. Lemaître, qui a été si bienveillant à cette petite soirée, plus que bienveillant même, m'avait fait demander un Mérimée et un Voltaire." [22] In fact Lemaître had said: "C'est à ne plus oser écrire; non seulement c'est extraordinaire, mais cela fait peur." [23]

The Dreyfus Affair caused strained feelings between them. Like Barrès, Lemaître was an anti-Dreyfusard and ceased to frequent salons such as Mme Straus's, where he was most likely to encounter Proust. In view of Proust's strong feelings regarding the Dreyfus case, it is not hard to imagine what a disappointment Lemaître's stand must have been for him. Their differences never affected Lemaître's genuine regard for Proust's talents, however. Proust often proudly quoted one of his words: "Ce Proust, quand c'est mal, c'est aussi bien que Dickens, et quand c'est bien, c'est beaucoup mieux." [24]

[19] *Correspondance générale,* IV, 53.
[20] Dreyfus, *Souvenirs sur Marcel Proust,* p. 59.
[21] *Correspondance générale,* IV, 225.
[22] *Ibid.,* I, 210.
[23] See Maurois, *À La Recherche de Marcel Proust,* p. 98.
[24] *Ibid.,* p. 319.

Emile Zola

Proust's refined taste disposed him against Zola and his works. To the Comtesse de Noailles he wrote apropos of her *Visage émerveillé*: "Et sans vouloir forcer et vulgariser une nuance jusqu'à en faire de ce livre un *Rougon-Macquart!* . . ." [25] In spite of Proust's ardent Dreyfusism, Zola's part in the Affair did not incline him more favorably. The reference to the author of *J'accuse* is wholly belittling. To praise another defender of Dreyfus, Proust wrote Mme Straus: "Il a bien plus fait que Zola." [26]

In matters of esthetics Proust and Zola are basically incompatible. Proust eyed literary schools and theories always with suspicion. Even as a young man he had written: "Je pense . . . que toute ces écoles littéraires qui prétendent ruiner la précédente ne valent pas grand'chose. La raison, je pense, c'est qu'elles se font une idée trop matérielle de la souveraineté littéraire." [27] For Proust, the writer was the translator of an inner vision. His art must not be yoked to a program or a system or anything, in fact, that might detract from that inward contemplation. Proust warned against "la grossière tentation pour l'écrivain d'écrire des œuvres intellectuelles. Grande indélicatesse. Une œuvre où il y a des théories est comme un objet sur lequel on laisse la marque du prix." [28]

Proust's concept of artistic creation precludes the possibility of any sympathy toward the realistic—or naturalistic—method: "La littérature qui se contente de 'décrire les choses,' de donner un misérable relevé de leurs lignes et de leur surface est, malgré sa prétention réaliste, la plus éloignée de la réalité." [29] Zola the theorist and chief of a school must have disturbed Proust fully as much as Zola the vulgar and pretentious writer living on publicity and *succès de scandale.*

Paul Bourget

Marcel Proust's first contacts with Paul Bourget were through Laure Hayman, the celebrated courtesan of the times, who furnished some of the features of Odette de Crécy in *À La Recherche du temps perdu.* Young Proust was the darling of this singular person. She took him everywhere with her, calling him "mon petit Marcel" or "mon petit Saxe psychologique." When Paul Bourget made her the heroine of his novel *Gladys Harvey,* she made Proust a present of the book, bound in a piece of her silk petticoat. Marcel requested her to convey his great admiration to the author. Bourget replied:

[25] *Correspondance générale,* II, 91. [26] *Ibid.,* VI, 50. [27] *Ibid.,* IV, 182.
[28] *Le Temps retrouvé,* II, 26-27. [29] *Ibid.,* p. 36.

Votre Saxe psychologique, le petit Marcel, comme vous l'appelez, est tout simplement exquis si j'en juge d'après cette lettre que vous avez eu la gracieuse idée de m'envoyer. Sa remarque sur le passage de *Gladys* concernant Jacques Molon prouve un esprit qui sait penser sur ses lectures, et tout son enthousiasme m'a fait chaud à sentir. Dites-le-lui, et qu'une fois sorti du travail auquel je suis attelé j'aurais un grand plaisir à le rencontrer. Puisque son père lui a donné trois conseils, et vous un quatrième, je lui en donnerai, moi, un cinquième: celui de ne pas laisser s'éteindre en lui cet amour des lettres qui l'anime. Il cessera d'aimer mes livres parce qu'il les aime trop. Claude Larcher sait trop bien que trop aimer, c'est être à la veille de désaimer. Mais qu'il ne désaime pas cette beauté de l'art qu'il devine, qu'il cherche à travers moi, indigne. Et, quoique ce conseil passant par la bouche d'une Dalila soit comme une ironie, dites-lui qu'il travaille, et développe tout ce que porte en elle sa déjà si jolie intelligence.[30]

Bourget's prophecy regarding his own work was correct, for the only subsequent references in Proust to Bourget are disparaging. He considered him a snob author and contrasted his success with the lack of proper recognition suffered by writers of greater merit: "Mais les gens du monde sont si pénétrés de leur propre stupidité qu'ils ne peuvent jamais croire qu'un des leurs a du talent. Ils n'apprécient que les gens de lettres qui ne sont pas du monde. Seulement (c'est encore un effet de leur stupidité) ils n'apprécient les gens de lettres que s'ils expriment leur mentalité à eux gens du monde. Ils trouvent les livres de Mme de Noailles stupides et ceux de Bourget sublimes." [31] Again Proust bursts forth on the stupidity of people in general and lashes Paul Bourget: "Du reste je suis étonné de voir ce que des gens même très intelligents admirent et approuvent. Par exemple un discours de Bourget où sont cités les calembours dignes de L... et où il y a une profession de foi d'antisémitisme qu'il aurait été en tous cas plus délicat de garder pour lui-même si elle est sincère puisqu'il a eu ce malheur pour un antisémite d'être lancé par un juif, doté par une juive et d'épouser une convertie." [32] Anti-Semitism is the one social issue that would set Proust's blood boiling.

Here with Bourget, as with Boylesve and others, we see that Proust's evaluations of an author have stood the test of time. Little is left of the prestige that Bourget enjoyed at the height of his career. Often Proust's desire to be agreeable renders his remarks on an author valueless as a critical estimate. But personal antipathy does not seem to have destroyed his sense of values. He was able to be fair to Barrès and others against whom he could feel personal grievance. His real quarrel with Bourget, although we have little information on the subject, would appear to rest upon esthetic convictions, the basis on which he judged and found also wanting Zola and, as we shall see, Charles Péguy.

[30] Collection Daniel Halévy. See Maurois, pp. 42-43.
[31] *Correspondance générale*, VI, 97.
[32] *Ibid.*, p. 91.

Francis Jammes

Francis Jammes captivated Proust as he had captivated all literary Paris. From 1892 on, when Jammes sent his little volume simply entitled *Vers* to Mallarmé, Gide, and Régnier, his genius was acclaimed by even the most divergent literary factions. Book publishers solicited his works and periodicals invited his collaboration. From time to time insistent invitations from persons such as Loti, Daudet, and Gide persuaded him to forsake his provincial retreat. A public surfeited with Parnassian splendor and Symbolist hermeticism found Jammes's naïve verses thoroughly refreshing.

Proust greeted the new poet in his article on the *Eblouissements* of Mme de Noailles (1907) by including his among the Six Gardens of Paradise. Jammes's garden we recognize as that of the hare in *Le Roman du lièvre.* In this book Proust could note Jammes's interest in botany and his habit of turning to nature for pious inspiration:

> Rien . . . ne semble d'abord plus près de la nature que le divin jardin de Francis Jammes, de toute façon un vrai jardin du Paradis, puisque le poète lui-même nous en a dit, de ce jardin, qu'il était au Paradis semblable exactement à ce qu'il est sur la terre: à la même place, pas bien loin de la plaque en fonte bleue qui indique: "Castétis à Balansun, cinq kilomètres," entouré de prairies "dont l'émail sertit des lacs de saphir et que bornent les glaçons bleus des Pyrénées," plein de lis communs, de grenadiers, de choux avec les deux petits chats gris qu'il a le plus aimés sur la terre, et ce laurier dont les enfants viennent au jour des Rameaux, cueillir une branche à laquelle ils enfilent des oranges, des dragées, des fleurs en papier et des oiseaux en pain d'épice. Mais la beauté des fleurs n'y semble pas toujours suffire au poète. Il y ajoute la dignité que leur donne d'avoir paru dans l'Ecriture et d'avoir été préférées par Dieu. Et lui aussi fait de la botanique. Il sème des oxalis pour étudier le sommeil des végétaux, et sa botanique tourne vite à la théologie, à l'astrologie, à des systèmes du monde, d'ailleurs de parti pris très simples, comme chez son "vieux Jean de La Fontaine."
>
> Dieu fait bien ce qu'il fait; sans en chercher la preuve,
> Dans le "papillon aurore" je la treuve.[33]

Whenever Proust had occasion to mention Jammes, he praised him highly. Phrases in his letters, such as "l'écrivain que j'admire le plus,"[34] "que je place au-dessus de tous,"[35] "émerveillement devant son œuvre,"[36] demonstrate how great his admiration was. With typical self-effacement, Proust demurred when his name was placed as high as Jammes's[37] and declared apropos of an article in which both names were

[33] *Chroniques,* pp. 184-85.
[34] Robert, *Comment Débuta Marcel Proust,* p. 39.
[35] *Correspondance générale,* IV, 65.
[36] Robert, *Comment Débuta Marcel Proust,* p. 45.
[37] *À Un Ami,* p. 143.

discussed that he could not enjoy a favorable comment on his own work by a writer unsympathetic toward Jammes.[38] Proust let it be known that he found it highly unjust that Jammes was not made an Academician.[39] With all due allowance for Proustian hyperbole, his esteem for Jammes seems thoroughly genuine. He was therefore quite gratified by Jammes's praise for his own work. The hyperboles were apparently not only on Proust's side. To Jean-Louis Vaudoyer Proust wrote with delight: "Je reçois une lettre de Francis Jammes où il m'égale à Shakespeare et à Balzac!"[40] He thought seriously of sending this letter to the papers. In 1916, when the publication of subsequent volumes of *À La Recherche du temps perdu* seemed near at hand, Proust felt deep concern over Jammes's possible reaction, fearing the effect they might have on Jammes's religious and moral sensibilities.[41] His high regard for Jammes made Proust look forward with great pleasure to making his personal acquaintance.

When at last Proust did meet Jammes, he felt the same dismay experienced by Gide and others. Gide had been so startled by Jammes's outlandish appearance that he left off using the *tu* by which they were wont to address each other in letters. Proust's first encounter with Jammes must have occurred during the war years at the time of one of Jammes's infrequent trips to Paris. In 1918 Proust dined with him at the Daudets'. He wrote shortly afterwards: "J'ai reçu l'autre jour des choses de Jammes que je trouve admirables, et je sens que je l'admire bien plus que ne font les jamistes. A lui-même, je ne m'habitue pas très bien."[42]

Although Proust, as a perfect esthete, was pained when the beauty of a work was not borne out in the artist,[43] Jammes's poetry held for him too many charms to let his impression of the man alter his feelings toward the work. Probably Jammes's success with writers Proust admired would have been enough to dispose him favorably— going along with the right people was very important to Proust. But there were other and deeper appeals for him in Jammes.

It is significant that Proust's first mention of Jammes is in connection

[38] Robert, *Comment Débuta Marcel Proust,* pp. 45-46.

[39] *Correspondance générale,* VI, 101.

[40] *Ibid.,* IV, 64.

[41] Proust, *Lettres à André Gide* (Ides et Calendes, 1949), p. 53. As a matter of fact, Jammes had ardently begged him to leave out a scene between the two girls in *Swann.* (*Correspondance générale,* III, 69.)

[42] Lucien Daudet, *Autour De Soixante Lettres de Marcel Proust,* p. 215.

[43] One would think Proust actually had Jammes in mind when he wrote: "Dans notre triste époque, sous nos climats, les poètes, j'entends les poètes hommes, dans le même moment où ils jettent sur les champs en fleurs un regard extasié, sont obligés en quelque sorte . . . de s'exclure, par l'imagination, du paysage. Ils sentent que la grâce dont ils sont environnés s'arrête à leur chapeau melon, à leur barbe, à leur binocle." *Chroniques,* pp. 179-80.

with gardens. In Jammes he could find a poet who shared his great love of flowers and countryside. The man who stood in raptures before a hawthorn hedge found a kindred soul in the author of *Le Roman du lièvre*. This book gave Proust the same ecstasy that he experienced before a scene of flowering trees. He abandoned himself voluptuously in Jammes's simple, natural world, so different from his own artificial environment. "On aime toujours un peu à sortir de soi, à voyager, quand on lit." [44] Forbidden for causes of health almost all contact with nature, and, spiritually, confined by his intelligence, his lucidity, and his conscience, Proust found a release in the instinctive world created by other writers. Robert Brasillach, who relates how Proust wept over Colette's stories of naïve and happy existences, concludes: "Cet homme trop fin, intelligent, malheureux, avait les mêmes rêves que les écrivains qui se font de Tahiti un paradis imaginaire parce qu'ils ont vu des toiles de Gauguin. Ce qu'il lui faut, c'est la vie simple." [45] Proust felt with all his heart that in staying close to nature Jammes was staying close to the greatest of all sources of artistic inspiration. Years before his evocation of Jammes's garden, in "Contre l'Obscurité," he had exhorted poets to turn back directly to nature for their inspiration: "Que les poètes s'inspirent plus de la nature, où, si le fond de tout est un et obscur, la forme de tout est individuelle et claire. Avec le secret de la vie, elle leur apprendra le dédain de l'obscurité. Est-ce que la nature nous cache le soleil, ou les milliers d'étoiles qui brillent sans voiles, éclatantes et indéchiffrables aux yeux de presque tous? Est-ce que la nature ne nous fait pas toucher, rudement et à nu, la puissance de la mer ou du vent d'ouest?" [46] The entire essay reads like an endorsement of Jammes's esthetic of simplicity and submission to nature. Although Proust claims not to have read Jammes before 1906,[47] it is not impossible that talk of him had already reached his ears and that the example of the poet of Orthez might have encouraged Proust to attack the obscurantists of the day.

Jammes, in close contact with nature, had found an expression that betrayed none of the authenticity of his sentiments. This is what Proust noted in his article "Vacances de Pâques," published in *Figaro* (1913). After ruminating the problem of the relationship between art and life, Proust attempts to define a fundamental task of the writer: "C'est une des tâches du talent de rendre aux sentiments que la littérature entoure d'une pompe conventionnelle leur tour véridique et naturel; ce n'est pas une des choses que j'admire le moins dans l'*Annonce faite à Marie*, de

[44] "Journées de lecture," *Pastiches et mélanges*, p. 268.

[45] Cited by Maurois, p. 146.

[46] *Chroniques*, p. 143.

[47] Professor Philip Kolb informs us that, in an unpublished letter of 1906 to Fernand Gregh, Proust speaks of having just read some Jammes for the first time.

Paul Claudel,—n'est-ce pas à ceux qui s'extasient devant la gloire des tympans de savoir goûter la finesse des quatre feuilles—que les bergers, le soir de Noël, ne disent pas: ' Noël, voici le Rédempteur '; mais: ' Kiki, il fait froué.' . . . Dans l'œuvre admirable du grand poète Francis Jammes, je trouverais bien d'autres exemples de ce genre." [48]

In his own work Proust strove to keep language free from embellishment. Whether Françoise or Charlus, each character expresses himself in a language that is his alone. The author limits his own part to elucidation and commentary, furnishing, as it were, a translation of the character's speech. For Proust, like Bergson, believed that language is a revelation of the *moi profond* of an individual. Its voice can be heard in turns of phrases, emphasis, all the idiosyncrasies of one's speech. Bent upon exposing this essential personality, the "véridique et naturel" self, Proust guarded against putting any veil of literary conventionality over the characteristic expression of sentiments and attitudes. He wrote to Camille Vettard: "Quant au style, je me suis efforcé de rejeter tout ce que dicte l'intelligence pure, tout ce qui est rhétorique, enjolivement et, à peu près, images voulues et cherchées . . . pour exprimer mes impressions profondes et authentiques et respecter la marche naturelle de ma pensée." [49]

Proust's foregoing statement brings us to the problem of craftsmanship versus inspiration, as we know, a major preoccupation with Proust. On the one hand, he was too intellectual, too conscious an artist himself, to deny the intelligence a role in a work of art (not even the Surrealists would identify the poem exactly with the dream). On the other hand, Proust knew that genius goes beyond skill and workmanship. Jammes's work prompted him to reflect further on the problem and try to formulate his views. In some way the two factors of artistic creation must be reconciled.

Craftsmanship, "tout ce que dicte l'intelligence pure" arouses Proust's general hostility. He attacks it usually in its basest form—correctness. One may wonder that an artist as sensitive and subtle should be so indifferent to flagrant violations of grammar and accepted standards of writing. Yet Proust is more annoyed than embarrassed when the flaws of his style are exposed, and he rises quickly to the defense of others accused of negligences. It is pertinent that his very favorite authors—Saint-Simon and Balzac—are famous for their carelessness.

In discussing Flaubert's style, Proust points out that even in the case of a very conscious artist there may be much incorrect writing: "Un bon élève, chargé de relire les épreuves de Flaubert, eût été capable d'en

[48] *Chroniques*, pp. 108-9.
[49] *Correspondance générale*, III, 195.

effacer bien des fautes." [50] He attributes to Flaubert his own feeling that grammatical correctness is at best a negative virtue, for Flaubert seems generally quite unconcerned about matters such as obscure antecedents or confusing syntax. However, when to achieve his desired expression he needs to be strict about grammar, no one is more scrupulously exact. One thing alone concerns him—what Proust calls the *rendu de sa vision*.[51] At times this vision may require the strictest observance of rule; at other times it may even demand the violation of conventional syntax: "Ces singularités grammaticales traduisant en effet une vision nouvelle, que d'application ne fallait-il pas pour bien fixer cette vision, pour la faire passer de l'inconscient dans le conscient, pour l'incorporer enfin aux diverses parties du discours!" [52] So incorrectness may not indicate carelessness at all, but rather a conscious effort to attain a desired artistic effect. We may conclude that Proust felt deviation from conventional standards of good writing either unimportant or fully justified. But in itself, incorrectness cannot constitute valid grounds for censure on an esthetic level. Proust restates his position in a letter to Jacques-Emile Blanche, written about the same time: "C'est à mon avis par une incompréhension absolue de ce qu'est le style qu'on croit que pureté de style a un rapport quelconque avec absence de fautes. L'absence de fautes est une qualité purement subalterne, nullement esthétique." [53]

These remarks, made toward the end of his life when his last words on the subject were being written, are already anticipated in what he said concerning Jammes. He wrote to Louis de Robert in 1913: "Ce que vous dites de Jammes est très vrai. Mais pour moi le plus précieux, ce ne sont pas ses meilleurs ouvrages. On appelle ainsi ceux où se sentent le moins ses défauts. Mais beaucoup de gens sans génie sont doués de ces qualités qui lui manquent et pourraient améliorer ses livres. L'absence de qualités que tant de gens possèdent ne saurait être bien grave." [54] The stand for spontaneous expression that Proust appears to take here does not, of course, mean to discredit painstaking artistic labor. Note his indignation that some of Musset's early verse might be prized more highly than his mature attainments. He stated in 1920: "Et nous devons mettre quelque scrupule, quelque conscience, dans notre appréciation des diverses œuvres d'un grand écrivain. Quand Musset, année par année, branche par branche, se hausse jusqu'aux *Nuits* . . . n'y a-t-il pas quelque cruauté à préférer aux premières:

[50] "A propos du 'Style' de Flaubert," *Chroniques*, p. 195.
[51] *Ibid.*, p. 196.
[52] *Ibid.*, p. 201.
[53] *Correspondance générale*, III, 168.
[54] Robert, *Comment Débuta Marcel Proust*, p. 40.

A Saint Blaise, à la Zuecca
Nous étions, nous étions bien aise." [55]

The year before, he had written to Blanche that to prefer a first version was to deny the organic process whereby an atom develops. But, he added, it was nevertheless possible that a first version might have a vitality that corrections destroy.[56] All these utterances indicate that, in spite of the great respect Proust felt for artistic achievement, he considered the essential version of a work of art to be the first, inspired one.

We have observed the distinction Proust made in the case of Flaubert between stylistic correctness and the exact expression of the inner vision. In connection with Jammes, we have evidence that Proust is willing to push his tolerance of incorrectness to all imperfections of literary structure. Form, as such, is not of primary importance: "Ne sût-il pas mettre ses sensations en ordre, faire un livre, même un conte, même un paragraphe, même une phrase, il lui resterait que la cellule même, l'atome, c'est-à-dire l'épithète et l'image sont chez lui d'une profondeur et d'une justesse que personne n'atteint." [57] The atom that he speaks of here and in the letter to Blanche is clearly for Proust the fundamental of the literary art—the epithet or the image. In the essay on Flaubert he states unequivocally: "la métaphore seule peut donner une sorte d'éternité au style. . . ." [58]

The image, as we know from the ample discussions in *À La Recherche du temps perdu,* is not for Proust an artificially created flower of rhetoric but an "inevitable" glimpse of the true and absolute nature of things. He goes on to suggest as much here:

> Au fond de nous nous sentons bien que les choses sont ainsi, mais nous n'avons pas la force d'aller jusqu'à ce fond extrême où gît la vérité, l'univers réel, notre impression authentique. Et nous ordonnons magnifiquement des à peu près d'expressions. Jammes, lui, laisse dans un grand désordre des expressions dont chacune est une révélation. Voilà pourquoi quand on dit qu'il est balbutiant, moi je trouve qu'il n'y a que lui qui parle net. Sans doute, j'aimerais mieux que toutes ces parcelles de vérité entrassent dans un ensemble admirable qui serait la révélation du monde réel. Mais j'aime mieux leurs justes indices que les grandes constructions où dix mille ratages, fondés sur l'intelligence et la rhétorique, donnent l'impression (pas à moi) d'une réussite.[59]

The image must be inevitable, the only one. Art conceived of as a metaphysical instrument, a means of probing the essential nature of things, cannot concern itself much with technique. The exactness demanded of a

[55] *Chroniques,* p. 209.
[56] See p. 56, n. 51.
[57] Robert, *Comment Débuta Marcel Proust,* p. 40.
[58] *Chroniques,* p. 193.
[59] Robert, *Comment Débuta Marcel Proust,* pp. 40-41.

writer is of a much deeper sort. To all appearances the work of a great artist may be careless and clumsy. This is not important. All his capacities must be mobilized to translate faithfully his deepest experiences: "Pour écrire ce livre essentiel, le seul livre vrai, un grand écrivain n'a pas, dans le sens courant, à l'inventer puisqu'il existe déjà en chacun de nous, mais à le traduire. Le devoir et la tâche d'un écrivain sont ceux d'un traducteur." [60] He is aware of the presence within him of "une réalité éternelle, intuitivement perçue par l'inspiration." [61] The talent which is his must be consecrated to giving artistic form to this reality. It is only here that the conscious efforts of the writer are properly employed. To use them trivially for other aims and effects (didacticism, rhetoric, embellishment, virtuosity, etc.) is to betray his most serious and exalted mission. Writing thus under the dictation of nature, the first duty of the artist is "de ne rien ajouter de son propre cru à ce message divin." [62]

This is Proust's resolution of the problem of inspiration versus technique. He finds a place for craftsmanship, but only in the service of inspiration, with very specific duties to perform. With technique as we usually think of it, he has little concern. The main tenets of his mature esthetic—the essential data of art, its function, the proper office of the artist—are already indicated in his appreciation of Francis Jammes. He seemed to glimpse in the works of this poet an illustration of his own views. Jammes's uncompromising art gave Proust courage and incited him to formulate a defense of spontaneity in art that anticipates the revolutionary manifestoes of the 1920's and '30's.

Charles Péguy

En principe un art où un mot en appelle un autre, selon la loi de l'association des idées . . . où une chose est redite dix fois en laissant le choix entre 10 formules dont aucune n'est la vraie, est pour moi le contraire de l'art.

Thus Proust wrote to Lucien Daudet in 1914 after reading Péguy.[63] He had already written to Louis de Robert the year before in the same vein: "Quant à certaines proses, comme celle de M. Péguy, par exemple, où règnent un état d'esprit qui est exactement le contraire de l'inspiration et de la solidification artistique, une espèce d'indolence au cours de laquelle un mot vous en fait imaginer un autre, et où on n'a pas le courage de sacrifier ses tâtonnements." [64] And to Léon Daudet he explained: ". . . si je suis un peu injuste pour Péguy c'est surtout parce que dire

[60] *Le Temps retrouvé,* II, 37.
[61] "En Mémoire des églises assassinées," *Pastiches et mélanges,* pp. 154-55.
[62] *Ibid.,* p. 156.
[63] Lucien Daudet, p. 108.
[64] Robert, *Comment Débuta Marcel Proust,* p. 41.

trois fois à peu près une chose me semble n'avoir aucun rapport avec la dire une fois telle qu'elle est. La vérité, même littéraire, n'est pas le fruit du hasard, et on pourrait s'asseoir devant son piano pendant 50 ans et essayer toutes les combinaisons de notes sans trouver telle divine phrase de tel grand musicien. Je crois que la vérité (littéraire) se découvre à chaque fois comme une *loi* physique. On la trouve ou on ne la trouve pas." [65] Toward Péguy, Proust is as rigorous in his insistence upon artistic exactitude as were the seventeenth-century literary legislators. He acts like the "véritable ami" of Boileau's *Art poétique:*

> Un sage ami, toujours rigoureux, inflexible,
> Sur vos fautes jamais ne vous laisse paisible;
> Il ne pardonne point les endroits négligés;
> Il renvoie en leur lieu les vers mal arrangés;
> Il réprime des mots l'ambitieuse emphase;
> Ici, le sens le choque, et plus loin, c'est la phrase;
> Votre construction semble un peu s'obscurcir;
> Ce terme est équivoque, il le faut éclaircir,
> C'est ainsi que vous parle un ami véritable.

The transformation of the material of inspiration into art implies painstaking application and expert craftsmanship, we are informed. In Péguy's work there seems no evidence of either. As Proust asserted in connection with Claudel,[66] an artist must know how to choose and reject, and to publish rough drafts or early versions is utterly "insensé." No "à peu près" expressions, as he would speak of them in connection with Paul Morand, will do. Until a writer has found the unique, the "inévitable," word to translate his vision, he should continue to work in silence.

Proust's severity toward Péguy may cause surprise in the light of his generosity and sympathy for the spontaneous art of Francis Jammes. There is, however, no real inconsistency. The indulgence Proust felt toward Jammes was for violations of rules and of language conventionalities; his censure of Péguy is based on the latter's failure to reject expressions that imperfectly or only partially expressed his inspiration. "Dans tous les arts, il semble que le talent soit un rapprochement de l'artiste vers l'objet à exprimer, tant que l'écart subsiste, la tâche n'est pas achevée. . . ." [67]

Proust was touched by the hardships of Péguy's life and by his heroic death; yet he could never bring himself to admire his work. For years the *Cahiers de la Quinzaine* piled up in his apartment. He had subscribed to them merely to please Daniel Halévy, who admired Péguy fervently.

[65] "Des Lettres inédites de Marcel Proust," présentées par Henri Mondor, *Bulletin de la Société des Amis de Marcel Proust,* II (1952), 15.

[66] See p. 56, n. 51 ff.

[67] Proust, Preface to Morand, *Tendres Stocks,* pp. 22-23.

After reading the first *Cahier,* Proust wrote his old friend: "Je trouve ton ami sans talent pour telle et telle raison, mais puisqu'il est malheureux, je souscrirai quand même." [68]

His conviction of Péguy's worthlessness was so strong that it shook his faith in his own critical judgment. If Péguy's work be great, he decided with bitter discouragement, then his own esthetic values must be false and he must be incapable of discrimination. His friends—Lucien Daudet, Daniel Halévy—all praised Péguy. The collaborators of the *Nouvelle Revue Française* as well: "Je ne peux pas exprimer assez ma stupéfaction de voir que, dans des milieux intelligents, comme à la *Nouvelle Revue Française,* par example, on trouve cela admirable. . . . C'est ce qui fait quelquefois que je me demande si j'ai raison de publier ce livre, sentant que je suis sur les autres, par conséquent sur des points où j'ai chance d'être plus impartial, en si profond désaccord avec les moins bêtes de mes contemporains. Et je vous parle de la revue que je trouve la plus intelligente, la seule lisible." [69]

In spite of his misgivings, Proust remained adamant in his condemnation of Péguy. Usually his opinions of other writers are nuanced and difficult to pin down. In Péguy's case there can be no doubt. In his own words: "J'exècre la littérature du pauvre Péguy et n'ai jamais varié." [70] Péguy's prolixity and groping expression violated one of Proust's fundamental esthetic principles.

André Gide

It seems curious and sad that the two greatest French writers of this century should not have had more mutual understanding and appreciation. Proust and Gide, who both enjoyed the rare privilege of having their genius universally recognized in their lifetime, remained indifferent and suspicious before one another. Their occasional protests of admiration and good will cannot hide a fundamental disaccord. And this in spite of a community of cause and interests. The little Proust has to say in his letters regarding Gide's writing contrasts strikingly with the interest he shows in several authors of distinctly inferior gifts. Of course, much of Gide's work did not appear until after Proust's death. Proust did not know *Les Faux Monnayeurs* and the incomparable diaries. Excuses can be made for Gide, too. The fact remains, his rejection of *À La Recherche du temps perdu* in the name of the Nouvelle Revue Française stands as a monumental critical blunder.

As Proust was putting the finishing touches on his novel and turning

[68] *Correspondance générale,* III, 238.
[69] Robert, *Comment Débuta Marcel Proust,* pp. 41-42.
[70] *Correspondance générale,* III, 238.

his mind toward its publication, the N. R. F. appealed to him as the logical house to bring out his work. In spite of its youth, it already enjoyed a prestige to which a man who always insisted on the best in everything, who patronized only the most modish shops and knew the specialties of each, could not be indifferent. Not all its policies met with Proust's approval, he failed to share some of its enthusiasms, but after all its review was "la plus intelligente, la seule lisible." [71] He asked his friend Antoine Bibesco, who had presented him with a subscription to the *N. R. F.* a couple of years before, to approach the directors on his behalf. Prince Bibesco obligingly arranged a dinner party at which Proust could talk to Gide. For some reason the plan was not carried out. Perhaps Proust was unwell. Perhaps Gide refused to see Proust. To Jacques-Emile Blanche, who likewise was trying to be of service to Proust, he had replied: "Proust? Proust? N'est-ce pas lui qui écrit des articles dans *Le Figaro?* Un amateur? Un boulevardier?" [72] Proust had made an unfavorable impression upon him years before. He told him quite bluntly in the letter he would soon write: "Je m'étais fait de vous une image d'après quelques rencontres dans 'le monde,' qui remontent à près de vingt ans. Pour moi, vous étiez resté celui qui fréquente chez Mmes X. . . et Z. . ., celui qui écrit dans *Le Figaro*. . . . Je vous croyais—vous l'avouerai-je?—'du côté de chez Verdurin.'" [73] Gide did not trouble himself even to read the book. Leafing through, his eye fell upon a phrase that seemed to make further perusal unnecessary: "un front où des vertèbres transparaissent." [74] On the basis of this *lapsus*—and Gide's preconceived notion of the author—the publishers rejected *À La Recherche du temps perdu,* thus making, as Gide shortly had to admit, "la plus grave erreur de la N. R. F." [75]

It would be interesting to know all the circumstances surrounding Gide's famous letter apologizing to Proust for not having recognized the merit of his work. The available facts suggest great activity behind the scenes at the N. R. F.

One will remember that Proust's book was, after being turned down by Mercure de France, Fasquelle, and Ollendorff, as well as the N. R. F., finally accepted by Grasset, to be published at author's expense. *Swann* left the printer's in November, 1913. Gide's letter is dated two months

[71] See p. 81, n. 69. Proust does not seem to be quite honest with Robert, for he implies that the N. R. F. had offered to publish his book but his commitments elsewhere had caused him to refuse. He alludes mysteriously to another reason, too, but that must be explained "dans les conversations." Robert, *Comment Débuta Marcel Proust,* p. 52.

[72] Cited by Pierre-Quint, *Marcel Proust,* p. 97.

[73] *Lettres à André Gide,* p. 9. Gide's letter is dated January, 1914.

[74] *Ibid.,* p. 10.

[75] *Ibid.,* p. 9.

later. He heaps upon the book the most lavish praise and upon himself the bitterest reproaches for having refused it. Proust surpassed himself in his exquisite reply.[76] The exultancy of triumphing where long he had failed, tempered with the humiliation of remembered failure, fills him with a sublime tenderness toward his offender. He admits having been hurt, but mysteriously alludes to having been hurt by Gide more deeply in another way. Great joys are, however, built upon small disappointments. If he had been accepted by the N. R. F. he would never have known the pleasure of Gide's letter. This last is a typically Proustian flourish. In spite of the grand style and generous sentiments, in spite of the questionable veracity of his claim to have received flattering offers from other publishers for his book, it is probable that Proust was sincerely touched. Gide's admiration for Proust was also probably quite genuine. But was there no *arrière-pensée*? This letter is followed by a note explaining that a rumor has reached Gide that Proust is not under contract with Grasset for the other volumes of *À La Recherche du temps perdu*. And if that is true, the N. R. F. is willing to take over the work. Gide says that this report had just come to him the day before. He had returned from Florence to attend the board meeting of the N. R. F. that decided to make the offer "à l'unanimité et d'enthousiasme."[77] Gide and the N. R. F. were not the only ones to have a change of heart. If we are to believe Proust, Fasquelle was ready to bid for volumes two and three. It seems very possible that Gide's effusions may have been at least partly dictated by business considerations.[78] These letters open the period of greatest contact between the two writers. Gide, dazzled by the revelation of Proust's genius and eager to woo him into the fold of the N. R. F., effaced from his mind his former impression of Proust.

Numerous letters testify to a lively correspondence during 1914. The

[76] *Ibid.*, pp. 13-17.

[77] *Ibid.*, p. 12.

[78] Here is the story according to Pierre-Quint: "Si Henri Ghéon publia la note dont nous avons parlé, c'est que Jacques Rivière, directeur de la Nouvelle Revue Française, lui avait dit: Voici *Du Côté de chez Swann*, un roman que notre maison d'édition a refusé. L'auteur écrit dans *Le Figaro*, fréquente chez Mme X et Z. Lisez-le cependant. . . .

"Lorsqu'il eut achevé sa lecture, Ghéon revint 'emballé' auprès de Rivière. Il l'incita, avec empressement, insistance et chaleur à entrer lui-même dans l'ouvrage. C'est alors que Jacques Rivière . . . à son tour il parla à André Gide de cette source, nouvelle pour lui, de création artistique. Gide reprit l'ouvrage sans parti pris. . . ." *Comment parut "Du Côté de chez Swann,"* p. 140.

"On comprend avec quels 'remords,' quelle 'honte' véritables les membres du groupe regrettaient leur examen trop superficiel du manuscrit de Proust. Maintenant qu'ils avaient lu le livre, ils échangeaient vivement entr'eux leurs impressions, leurs découvertes. L'ouvrage grandissait chaque jour à leurs yeux. . . . C'est à ce moment qu'André Gide ayant entendu dire qu'aucun traité. . . ." *Ibid.*, p. 145.

two writers discuss literature and send each other their books. Proust is following the adventures of Lafcadio in the pages of the *N.R.F.* He declares he has never waited for a fiction installment with such impatience! What will happen to the young woman whose purse Lafcadio has taken? He describes himself as "le captif anxieux et ravi" of the *Caves du Vatican.*[79] Why should this work have appealed to Proust so much? He had not cared very much for *Isabelle*[80] and has little to say about *L'Offrande lyrique,* Gide's translation of Tagore's work, which he has just received. It is chiefly the creation of Lafcadio. He *lives*! "Il faudrait dix lettres . . . pour vous faire comprendre le mal que m'a fait Cadio et c'est d'abord une preuve qu'il existe: 'je fais souffrir, donc je suis,'" Proust facetiously concludes.[81] In creating this character, nobody has been objective with so much perversity since Balzac wrote *Splendeurs et misères des courtisanes.* Proust, a Balzac lover, sees Cadio as a sort of Lucien de Rubempré. But Balzac was aided in inventing Lucien by a certain personal vulgarity whereas Gide's creation is wholly objective. All the more remarkable is Gide's achievement. It is a real creation, in the generative sense of Michelangelo—the creator is absent, he has done all and is not one of his creatures.[82]

Proust's remarks are only flattering phrases and cannot be taken as a serious effort to define or situate Gide's work. The incense they burn before each other becomes a bit thick. Gide has written begging Proust not to judge him on his *Caves.* The work has aged, he feels sure. Proust's pretty rejoinder is: "Qu'importe qu'elle ait vieilli pour vous, elle naît maintenant resplendissante et jeune dans nos pensées, laissez-la accomplir de cerveau en cerveau sa migration mystérieuse et que vous avez providentiellement réglée." [83] In turn, Proust begs him not to read the second volume of his novel which he has not had the strength to put in proper shape.

An odor less sweet but more penetrating than this flattery occasionally reaches Gide's nostrils. In his insidious way, Proust manages to suggest some rather disagreeable things to Gide. Lack of originality, poor construction, breach of good taste: these are accusations that anyone not drugged by fancy phrases could hear through these letters. One of the many "me's" reading the *Caves,* Proust coyly admits, made the idiotic mistake of not being able to see a criminal trying to evade justice without thinking of Dostoievski! Of course the other "me's" quickly corrected the erring one. Alas, one might say for Proust, the mischief is done!

[79] *Lettres à André Gide,* p. 24.

[80] See *À Un Ami,* p. 235. (Date of letter established by Philip Kolb as February, 1911. *La Correspondance de Marcel Proust.*)

[81] *Lettres à André Gide,* p. 33. [82] *Ibid.,* p. 26. [83] *Ibid.,* pp. 33-34.

In March Proust praises unreservedly the composition of the *Caves du Vatican* "dont les épisodes convergent, composés comme dans une rose d'Eglise." [84] In April he sneaks in this criticism: "Le point d'interrogation, la pointe de soleil levant et d'espoir sur lesquels s'achève votre livre, n'est peut-être pas, au point de vue purement géométrique de la composition, tout à fait satisfaisant. On s'attendait à ce que les issues fussent plus complètement bouchées, à avoir un livre hermétiquement clos." Then quickly withdraws it: "Mais il m'intéresse plus ainsi, faisant sa part à une des lois qui m'intéressent le plus, et que pour ma part je tâche toujours de mettre en lumière quand j'écris, à savoir les différences de pression, les variations de l'atmosphère morale pour un même individu. Cette aurore tonique de la fin me plaît beaucoup par là." [85] Alas, again the mischief is done.

Proust protests against passages of distasteful realism. His fastidiousness revolts at the picture of poor Fleurissoire plagued with pimples he fears may be venereal, squeezing his sores and rubbing them with saliva. "Moi, je ne peux pas, peut-être par fatigue, ou paresse, ou ennui, relater, quand j'écris, quelque chose qui ne m'a pas produit une impression d'enchantement poétique, ou bien où je n'ai pas cru saisir une vérité générale. Mes personnages n'enlèvent jamais leur cravate." But Proust concedes that he is probably in error: "Cet effort que je suis obligé de faire en suivant Fleurissoire chez le pharmacien, Balzac longtemps me l'imposa, et la réalité, la vie." [86]

What seems particularly worthy of note in Proust's remarks is not the validity of his criticism or even the interesting references to his own work. It is rather his way of introducing unobtrusively into his praise some rather damning comments. He is not so enamored of Gide's works as a quick reading of his letters might lead one to suppose. The reasons for Proust's attitude are, although consistent with his generally professed esthetic views, highly tinged with personal feeling. Proust and Gide disliked and distrusted one another and, in spite of great urbaneness, were violently jealous. Even in this period of their greatest rapport, they remained basically inimical.

It is of course very unfortunate that most of the letters Gide wrote Proust have never been found. They would throw useful light on the personal matters to which Proust keeps alluding. We should know exactly what he meant when he wrote: "Maintenant que vous avez bien senti . . . que mes sentiments pour vous ne sont que de reconnaissance, d'affection, d'admiration j'oserai, dans la douceur du tête-à-tête où les paroles peuvent faire subir les retouches nécessaires aux paroles précédentes et n'ont pas le caractère impitoyablement définitif et *ne varietur*

[84] *Ibid.*, p. 25. [85] *Ibid.*, p. 35. [86] *Ibid.*, pp. 25-26.

d'une lettre, vous confesser un grief que j'avais contre vous et qu'a tellement effacé votre adorable bonté." [87] Proust still betrays, however, a certain uneasiness toward Gide. It is apparent in such chiding words as the following: "Par exemple, vous persistez à me dire 'mon cher Proust,' et jamais (à défaut du prénom que je n'ose demander) 'cher ami.' Et vous avez mille fois raison si vous trouvez que le mot d'amitié excède un peu vos sentiments." [88] This is excessive, even with Proust, whose sensitivity was painfully acute with all his friends. In contrast to the cautious and coquettish Proust, we can imagine a bearish Gide, attracted and yet repelled by the personality of Marcel Proust. His ambivalent feelings led him to unburden himself to Proust concerning his personal life and his troubles, but without ever giving him full confidence.

His letters throw Proust in a flutter. From his bedroom Proust mobilizes all his forces to put them at his friend's disposal. Immediate travel, personal intervention, everything Proust can think of, he offers this friend whom he has not seen for twenty-two years! Although burning with curiosity, he protests his complete discretion, his usual indifference to other persons' problems, and entreats Gide to tell him all: "Je suis l'être le moins curieux et le moins indiscret qui soit. Quand on veut me faire une confidence, je l'arrête si je le peux. Mais. . . ." [89] Proust becomes so eager to help that he tells Gide in all seriousness that if he had but known Swann, he could have arranged things between him and Odette! His letter, overflowing onto the envelope, was followed by a gift of roses and tender verses from Villiers de l'Isle-Adam.

Proust's protests did not prevent Gide from accusing him openly of indiscretion. From the second letter, written four years later, but very much like the first, I take this: "Quant au défaut que vous m'attribuez—et qui est le plus contraire à ma nature!—l'indiscrétion. . . ." [90] It is comic and touching to observe Proust ransacking his memory for an incident that would explain Gide's misinterpretation. What trouble he gave himself to find favor with Gide!

In spite of Gide's reticence, Proust confided his own sorrows freely. The death of Agostinelli had plunged Proust into the darkest grief. He wrote to Gide with touching words: "Vous êtes trop bon de penser aussi à mes ennuis et à mes chagrins; hélas, la mesure a été comblée par la mort d'un jeune homme que j'aimais probablement plus que tous mes amis puisqu'elle me rend si malheureux. . . . C'était un garçon d'une intelligence délicieuse; et ce n'est pas du reste du tout pour cela que je l'aimais. J'ai été longtemps sans m'en apercevoir, moins longtemps que lui d'ailleurs." [91] When it was, however, a question of a real service Proust

[87] *Ibid.*, p. 22. [88] *Ibid.*, p. 59. [89] *Ibid.*, p. 28.
[90] *Ibid.*, p. 67. [91] *Ibid.*, pp. 38-39.

could perform for Gide, he excused himself in a manner well known to all readers of the correspondence. Gide has apparently suggested Proust do an article on the *Caves* for *Figaro,* the very paper he had spoken of so contemptuously. Proust replies that he has no more influence there, that he hasn't received the *Caves,* etc. Moreover, his grief at losing his friend is such, he declares, that he is "incapable d'écrire en ce moment un article, malgré l'honneur que ce serait pour moi de parler des *Caves* et la reconnaissance que je vous aurais de me le permettre." [92]

Need we other proof that all the mutual assurances of esteem and affection are just formalities when we remember that these two men, both living in Paris, have not met since 1892? Granted Proust's state of health, his excuse and pretext for not receiving Gide, he did have numerous other guests and he himself managed to get out more frequently than we once supposed. It was not until 1916 that the reunion finally took place. Gide entered it in his journal with exasperating terseness. "Achevé la soirée chez Marcel Proust (que je n'avais pas revu depuis 92). Je me promettais de raconter longuement cette visite; mais je n'y ai plus cœur ce matin." [93]

Back on calling terms, Gide paid at least several visits to Proust's apartment. By this time Proust was too sick or too busy to pay much attention to Gide. Note his letter which Professor Kolb tells us was written December 21, 1917: "Je vous remercie mille fois de m'avoir fait inviter chez Madame Raoul Duval. J'ai beaucoup regretté de ne pouvoir assister à cette soirée. Mais vous savez combien je me lève peu. Puis, j'avais cru que c'était une matinée. Quand la carte m'est retombée sous les yeux, j'ai reconnu mon erreur. . . ." [94] Proust seems much less anxious about the impression he would make on others. Gide, however, betrays an increasing jealousy of Proust. He suspected his malady of being just a feint: "Longtemps j'ai pu douter si Proust ne jouait pas un peu de sa maladie pour protéger son travail." [95] He tortured himself by comparing Proust's work with his own. "J'ai voulu me ratteler aux Mémoires," he wrote in 1918, "mais je n'y ai plus goût; les quelques passages que j'en ai lus à haute voix devant M. R. m'ont déçu; et la comparaison que j'en faisais avec les pages du merveilleux livre de Proust que je relisais d'autre part, achevait de m'accabler." [96] In time, he recovered enough to formulate a criticism in which one can see everything but artistic conviction: "La minutie de Proust peut amuser l'esprit. . . . Mais . . . l'art ne se satisfait point d'une si minutieuse et tatillonnante vérité." [97] One

[92] *Ibid.*, p. 43.
[93] Gide, *Oeuvres complètes* (Gallimard, 1932-39), VIII, 223.
[94] *Lettres à André Gide*, p. 47.
[95] Gide, *Oeuvres complètes*, X, 517.
[96] *Ibid.*, IX, 418.
[97] Cited by Pierre-Quint, *Comment parut "Du Côté de chez Swann,"* p. 106.

doubts if Gide ever cured his chronic jealousy. Years later he complained peevishly: "Curieux qu'on fasse tant de raffut pour les fautes d'impression dans les livres de Proust, qui écrivait au courant de la plume—et que, lorsqu'il s'agit d'un texte de moi dont chaque mot est pesé, l'on s'inquiète si peu de me citer exactement." [98]

Gide's most serious grievance against Proust concerned the subject of homosexuality. In 1921, the appearance of parts of *Sodome et Gomorrhe* in the *N. R. F.* brought about an open rupture. Gide declared the volume was an offense to truth, a cowardly subterfuge:

J'ai lu les dernières pages de Proust . . . avec, d'abord, un sursaut d'indignation. Connaissant ce qu'il pense, ce qu'il est, il m'est difficile de voir là autre chose qu'une feinte, qu'un désir de se protéger, qu'un camouflage, on ne peut plus habile, car il ne peut être de l'avantage de personne de le dénoncer. Bien plus: cette offense à la vérité risque de plaire à tous: aux hétérosexuels dont elle justifie les préventions et flatte les répugnances; aux autres, qui profiteront de l'alibi et de leur peu de ressemblance avec ceux-là qu'il portraiture. Bref, la lâcheté générale aidant, je ne connais aucun écrit qui, plus que la *Sodome* de Proust, soit capable d'enfoncer l'opinion dans l'erreur.[99]

He compared Proust with Wilde, another whom Gide treated badly, saying that both had made of a lie a work of art.[100]

Vis-à-vis Proust, whom he calls that master of dissimulation, Gide assumed an attitude of simplicity and forthrightness. The letters to Mme de Noailles outraged his sense of honesty:

Ces lettres de Proust à Mme de Noailles discréditent le jugement (ou la sincérité) de Proust bien plus qu'elles ne servent à la gloire de la poétesse. La flagornerie ne peut être poussée plus loin. Mais Proust connaissait assez Mme de N., la savait vaine et incapable de critique assez pour espérer que la louange la plus outrée lui paraîtrait la plus méritée, la plus sincère; il jouait d'elle comme il jouait de tous. Et je vois dans ses flatteries éhontées moins d'hypocrisie qu'un besoin maniaque de servir à chacun ce qui peut lui être le plus agréable, sans plus aucun souci de véracité, mais bien seulement d'opportunisme et surtout un désir d'épanouir et d'amener à se livrer celui sur qui il souffle de son plus chaud.[101]

Gide does not comment when he himself was served from the same dish. Note Proust's rhapsodic panegyric for the *Nourritures terrestres:* "Ces *Nourritures terrestres* qui ont déjà alimenté une génération et sur lesquelles bien d'autres vivront. Car le grand écrivain, et plus particulièrement vous, est comme la graine qui nourrit les autres de ce qui l'a nourrie

[98] Gide, *Oeuvres complètes,* XV, 417.

[99] *Ibid.,* X, 534.

[100] Note Proust's gentle chiding: " A ce propos, comme on doit la vérité amie même à Platon, j'ai trouvé que vous parliez sur un ton bien dédaigneux à Wilde. Je l'admire fort peu. Mais je ne comprends pas les réticences et les rudesses en parlant à un malheureux." *Lettres à André Gide,* p. 84.

[101] Gide, *Oeuvres complètes,* XV, 419-20.

d'abord elle-même. . . . Et cette idée, qui est une de celles que je me fais le plus volontiers de l'écrivain, prend, quand il s'agit de vous, quelque chose de si adéquat que c'est vrai comme à un degré de plus et sans comparaison." To flatter Gide, he goes on to speak slightingly of Claudel: "Mais qu'est-ce que c'est que les intentions artificielles de vers libre, ou je ne sais comment on appelle cela, de Claudel, à côté de cet accent des *Nourritures.* Vous vivrez car vous vous êtes laissé nourrir et vous avez nourri." [102]

Although Gide's sincerity threatened always to become professional, his attitude reveals how far apart these two champions of the same cause actually were. Gide could see salvation only outside of convention. Proust would work out a modus vivendi within the law. When Gide told him of his memoirs, Proust exclaimed, "Vous pouvez tout raconter . . . mais à condition de ne jamais dire: Je." Gide adds: "Ce qui ne fait pas mon affaire." [103] Not without reason Proust complained that Gide was a very difficult person.[104]

Gide decries Proust's "hypocrisy" for the harm it will do the cause of the Corydons. His work gives only a biased and partial picture of sexual inversion:

> Certains livres—ceux de Proust en particulier—ont habitué le public à s'effaroucher moins et à oser considérer de sang-froid ce qu'il feignait d'ignorer, ou préférait ignorer d'abord. Nombre d'esprits se figurent volontiers qu'ils suppriment ce qu'ils ignorent. . . . Mais ces livres, du même coup, ont beaucoup contribué, je le crains, à égarer l'opinion. La théorie de l'homme-femme, des "Sexuelle Zwischenstufen" . . . que lançait le Dr. Hirschfeld en Allemagne, assez longtemps déjà avant la guerre, et à laquelle Marcel Proust semble se ranger—peut bien n'être point fausse; mais elle n'explique et ne concerne que certains cas d'homosexualité, ceux dont précisément je ne m'occupe pas dans ce livre—les cas d'inversion, d'efféminement, de sodomie. . . . Ce que l'on a coutume d'appeler "l'amour grec": la pédérastie—qui ne comporte efféminement aucun, de part ni d'autre.[105]

Of the rancor Gide displayed over *Sodome et Gomorrhe,* a large part may be attributed to his feeling that Proust had stolen his show. Note the open letter to François Porché: "Ainsi vous signalez mon *Immoraliste*; mais ne parlez pas de *Saül,* bien plus topique assurément, publié en 1902, également, mais écrit cinq ans plus tôt. Il ne dépendait pas de moi que

[102] *Lettres à André Gide,* pp. 60-61.

[103] Gide, *Oeuvres complètes,* X, 514-16. Elsewhere Gide attributed the same word of caution to Wilde: "C'est là ce qui lui faisait dire: 'N'employez jamais *je.*'" *Ibid.,* XIV, 368.

[104] *Correspondance générale,* III, 246.

[105] Gide, *Oeuvres complètes,* IX, 178-79. One can imagine how indignant Proust would have been to have his study characterized thus. For he made for his work exactly the same claim as Gide for his. Proust writes: "C'est un caractère que je crois assez neuf, le pédéraste viril, épris de virilité, détestant les jeunes gens efféminés." *Lettres à la N.R.F.,* p. 103.

la pièce fût jouée; je fis ce que je pus pour la produire, Antoine faillit très courageusement m'y aider. . . . Je ne rappelle pas cela pour me targuer d'avoir devancé Proust, mais parce qu'il n'est pas dans mon humeur de jouer ce rôle du Moron de la farce, qui ne descend de son arbre pour combattre l'ours, qu'un autre ne l'ait préalablement mis par terre." [106] The failure of *Saül* was a bitter blow to Gide. Proust's condolences are perfunctory and do not indicate the least interest in the play itself.[107]

In perusing the letters and other documents bearing on the relationship between these men, we have found little of the fraternity and mutual appreciation that their genius and common interest might inspire. Rather have we found indifference, envy, mutual incomprehension. The last letters show that their relations never bettered. Proust acts, as usual, in a polite and conciliatory manner that does not hide a lack of interest. Gide is openly quarrelsome, accusing Proust of ingratitude toward the N. R. F., etc. In 1923 André Gide recorded a dream concerning Proust. It is a curious compensatory sort, laying quite bare Gide's notion of Proust and the antagonism he incited:

Rêvé cette dernière nuit:

Un domestique en livrée vint enlever sur un plateau les restes de la collation qui nous avait été servie. J'étais assis sur un simple escabeau, près d'un guéridon bas, à peu près au centre d'une vaste pièce peu éclairée. La personne avec qui je conversais, au visage à demi caché par les oreilles d'un grand fauteuil, était Marcel Proust. L'attention que je lui prêtais fut distraite par le départ du domestique, et je remarquai que celui-ci entraînait après lui un bout de ficelle, dont une extrémité se trouva dans ma main, tandis que l'autre alla se fixer entre les livres d'un rayon de la bibliothèque. Cette bibliothèque tapissait un des murs de la pièce. Proust y tournait le dos, tandis que j'y faisais face. Je tirai la ficelle et vis se déplacer légèrement deux gros vieux volumes somptueusement reliés. Je tirai un peu plus et les livres sortirent à demi du rayon, prêts à tomber; je tirai davantage encore, ils tombèrent. Le bruit de la chute me fit battre le cœur et coupa le récit que Proust était en train de faire. Je m'élançai vers la bibliothèque, ramassai l'un des livres, m'assurai que la reliure de maroquin plein n'était pas écornée; ce que je voulus aussitôt faire remarquer à mon ami pour le rassurer. Mais les plats étaient à demi détachés du dos et la reliure, somme toute, dans un état déplorable. Je compris intuitivement que Proust tenait beaucoup à ces livres; à celui-ci spécialement. Mais sur un ton d'amabilité exquise et tout à fait grand seigneur:

—Ce n'est rien. C'est une édition de Saint-Simon de. . . . Il me dit une date; et je reconnus aussitôt une édition des plus rares et des plus recherchées. Je voulais balbutier des excuses, mais Proust y coupant court commença de me montrer, avec force commentaires, quelques-unes des nombreuses illustrations du livre qu'il avait gardé sur ses genoux.[108]

It is regrettable not to be able to match this dream with one of Proust's.

[106] Gide, *Oeuvres complètes*, IX, 322-23.
[107] See *Lettres à la N. R. F.*, pp. 222, 226.
[108] Gide, *Oeuvres complètes*, XIII, 45 ff.

CHAPTER FOUR

The Younger Generation

De sa chambre close, il s'intéressait aux écrivains les plus jeunes, à Dada, aux trouvailles de Giraudoux, à la musique de Darius Milhaud, aux dessins de Picasso.[1]

For reasons of health and disposition, Proust advanced in years without ever ceasing to be young. His friends had matured, taken on families and situations. But Proust, shut in by his cork walls, had remained an adolescent, living chiefly back in the days when he was young. Estrangement from his contemporaries was inevitable. It was hard for him to recognize in the Academicians and diplomats the companions of his youth. The author of *À La Recherche du temps perdu* could find congenial associates and, in a sense, the friends of his youth, only in men a decade or more his junior.

With the passing of time and the spread of his own fame, Proust's relations with other writers had changed. The polite, respectful young man, sitting at the feet of his dear friends and masters, had become a master himself. He found the public for his new art not in Anatole France, Barrès, or Montesquiou, but in the younger generation. His art was the most precious part of his life, his very reason for being. He knew that his lifelong friends were too old, too prejudiced, to judge his work adequately. It belonged to the future. Before he died, he intended to make sure it was in the right hands. Moreover, to perpetuate and disseminate the views on literature which he had acquired through long reading and meditation he looked to budding talents. They were the ones to be converted to the truth as Proust saw it.

Hence for many reasons Proust abandoned his elders and contemporaries and turned to new writers. In the battle of the generations Proust took the side of the new. Even when he disagreed with new writers, he tried to be tolerant: "De jeunes écrivains, avec qui je suis d'ailleurs en sympathie, préconisent . . . une action brève avec peu de personnages. Ce n'est pas ma conception du roman." [1a] His tolerance was dictated, then, more by esthetic principle than by sentiment, by his conviction that art

[1] Pierre-Quint, *Marcel Proust,* p. 120.
[1a] Dreyfus, *Souvenirs sur Marcel Proust,* p. 287.

can never stand still but must keep creating new forms and viewpoints that replace the old. He wrote to Paul Morand: "Ce qui me désole, c'est de voir des gens . . . mettre le goût avant tout, ou du moins ce qu'ils nomment tel et nier d'avance tout ce que produiront les âges qui vont venir. Si Courbet, si Manet, si Renoir avaient été pénétrés d'une telle esthétique, nous n'aurions que Bouguereau. Ils ont fait classique parce qu'ils ont voulu faire nouveau." [2] Reconciled to the mutability of all things, Proust believed that art followed the general laws of nature. An art lives, changes, and dies like any other organism. It is replaced by a new vision of the world imposed by a new artist: "Et voici que le monde, qui n'a pas été créé une fois, mais l'est aussi souvent que survient un nouvel artiste, nous apparaît—si différent de l'ancien—parfaitement clair. . . . Tel est l'univers périssable et nouveau que crée l'artiste et qui durera jusqu'à ce qu'un nouveau survienne." [3] The new picture of things disturbs us and we hesitate to call its author great. Yet talent is precisely what renders possible this new vision: "Nous sommes très longs à reconnaître dans la physionomie particulière d'un nouvel écrivain le modèle qui porte le nom de 'grand talent' dans notre musée des idées générales. Justement parce que cette physionomie est nouvelle, nous ne la trouvons pas tout à fait ressemblante à ce que nous appelons talent. Nous disons plutôt originalité, charme, délicatesse, force; et puis un jour nous nous rendons compte que c'est justement tout cela le talent." [4] Thus Proust repudiated his master Anatole France, who had attacked the "école moderne," and championed the partisans of "singularité dans le style." The preface to Morand's *Tendres Stocks* constitutes Proust's reply to France.

Paul Morand

Morand was in the consular service in London when he first heard of Proust through Bertrand de Fénelon. It was in 1914, Morand tells us,[5] that Fénelon, having left his post in Oslo, stopped in London on his way home to volunteer for the army. Morand's curiosity was aroused by Fénelon's passionate description of *Swann* and its mysterious author. About a year later he met Proust under circumstances that in no way belied the mystery and eccentricity of the man whom Morand admits already admiring "éperdûment." Morand was occupying Henri Bardac's bachelor quarters in Paris at the time. One evening about eleven thirty he was roused by the doorbell. Proust had come to call. Thirty years later Morand vividly recalls his emotion as he stood in his pajamas before this

[2] See Paul Morand, "Notes," *Hommage à Marcel Proust*, p. 81.
[3] Preface to Morand, *Tendres Stocks*, pp. 34-35.
[4] *Du Côté de chez Swann*, I, 137.
[5] Morand, *Le Visiteur du soir* (Geneva: La Palatine, 1949), p. 13.

weird-looking individual bundled up in his garments of an outmoded elegance. The first conversation, which lasted far into the night, was chiefly a monologue, Proust talking of friends, of literature, and even of his own work. Toward dawn Proust climbed back into the taxi that had been waiting for him all the while. Thus began a friendship that lasted, in spite of Morand's frequent and prolonged absences from Paris, until another night in the rue Hamelin when Morand held watch over Proust's mortal remains.

The chief documents concerning the friendship between the ill and dying Proust and the young Morand beginning work in two careers are, of course, Proust's letters. They tell us very little, however, aside from recording dinner parties with titled and distinguished company. There are no literary discussions and little to indicate that their relationship was deeper than that of polite social intercourse. Yet this encounter of the aging Proust and the young writer must have been much more meaningful for them both. Early in December of 1917 Morand went to Rome as embassy secretary. His departure was for Proust a great blow. One can detect in his note to Morand a cry of real grief: "Je suis triste parce que vous partez. Plus triste encore parce que je sais que je vais vous oublier ou plutôt parce qu'un autre moi va venir, qui vous oubliera." [6] The war had bereft Proust of many friends. He had hoped to retain the faithful Morand, who cheered the sick man with his nocturnal visits: "Morand, parti hélas, rejoindre son poste à Rome comme secrétaire d'ambassade. Je le préférais au cabinet du Ministre d'où il pouvait quelquefois venir auprès de mon lit vers minuit, si je n'avais pas trop de crises, mes fumigations finies." [7] Too, Proust, obsessed by the ideas he develops in *À La Recherche du temps perdu*, that is, the multiplicity of the ego, the *intermittances du cœur*, felt that their friendship could never again be the same. The real tragedy in human relations is not that one will be forsaken, but that one will himself one day become indifferent. Proust develops this thought in a letter to the Princesse Soutzo: "J'ai un chagrin infini du départ de Morand, et peut-être plus encore de savoir que ce chagrin ne durera pas. . . . C'est de l'égoisme, c'est qu'on n'aime pas mourir à soi-même, être remplacé par un Proust inconnu de soi qui pourra fort bien se passer de Morand. Le Proust actuel n'est pas du tout comme cela. Je n'ai jamais tant aimé Morand que ce soir. Il y a eu entre nous, deux malentendus stupides qui ont paralysé un an d'amitié. Et maintenant sans explications, son départ, son absurde départ, éclairait tout." [8] We have in this letter the avowal of a misunder-

[6] "Notes," p. 81.
[7] Proust, *Lettres à Mme C.* (J. B. Janin, 1946), p. 169.
[8] *Le Visiteur du soir*, p. 70.

standing which, in itself, indicates that among the younger generation of writers Morand had a privileged place in Proust's heart.

On strictly literary grounds, Proust's admiration for Morand was not without certain reservations. To be sure he delighted in Morand's brilliant new vision, but he did not condone his affectations. Today the audacious up-to-date style of *Tendres Stocks* seems as quaint as a flapper's dress. The smart-aleck images offended Proust, whose esthetic was built upon reverence for the "inevitable" metaphor, the key to the mysteries of the universe. In the preface Gallimard asked him to write for *Tendres Stocks,* he remarks: "Le seul reproche que je serais tenté d'adresser à Morand, c'est qu'il a quelquefois des images autres que des images inévitables. Or, tous les à peu près d'images ne comptent pas." Proust's friendship with Morand tempered his criticism. In the same essay he feigns surprise that anyone could see the influence of Giraudoux in Morand's style. Yet he wrote to Jacques Boulenger, who had found *Clarissa* full of reminiscences: "Quant à ce que j'ai dit que Morand et Giraudoux ne se ressemblaient pas, je vous expliquerai de vive voix la raison d'amitié et de délicatesse qui m'a fait dire cela." [9]

Jean Giraudoux

Jean Giraudoux, Morand's precursor in "imagistic writing," attracted Proust from the first. His talents had been applauded generally by the literary elite since 1909 when Gide commented favorably on the *Provinciales.* His favor may account for the very hospitable reception Giraudoux enjoyed in the *N.R.F.*, where reviewers spoke highly of his works and Albert Thibaudet dedicated a flattering essay to him. In its pages Proust read the "Nuit de Châteauroux" and pronounced it "admirable." [10] He invited Giraudoux to call on him in his apartment, rue Laurent-Pichat.[11] It is interesting to remember that Giraudoux had so far produced none of his major works. *Suzanne et le Pacifique* would not appear until 1921, *Siegfried et le Limousin* a year later. On the basis of war sketches and adolescent reminiscences alone Giraudoux had created a select public of admirers not the least ardent of whom was Marcel Proust.

In 1920 Giraudoux was Proust's choice to succeed himself as a Goncourt winner: "Je considère Giraudoux comme l'auteur ayant atteint la plus étonnante réalisation, je veux dire comme étant le Prix Goncourt idéal de cette année." [12] Not everyone thought so highly of Giraudoux, how-

[9] *Correspondance générale,* III, 238.

[10] *Ibid.*, p. 193.

[11] See Porel, "Marcel Proust chez Réjane," p. 95.

[12] Jacques de Lacretelle, "Un Témoignage sur Proust," *Bulletin de la Société des Amis de Marcel Proust,* I (1950), 15.

ever, neither Lucien Daudet, whom Proust could not convince, nor the Académie Goncourt, which had refused Giraudoux before and would again this year. Proust consoles himself in defeat with Jacques Boulenger, who shared his admiration for the author of *Amica America*: "Comme vous avez raison sur Giraudoux! Il a un immense talent. Je suis crispé qu'on le reconnaisse si peu." [13]

The attention Proust paid to young writers is, of course, not proportionate to the value posterity or literary historians would place upon their works. Proust has most to say about those whom he knew personally. He never pretended to judge objectively or establish relative evaluations. We may regret Proust did not deal at length with Mauriac, Cocteau, and other writers who were to become great. But we are chiefly interested in learning about Proust himself, his taste and his esthetic attitudes as revealed through his comments on what he read. And for this, even inferior artists serve. Moreover, in Proust's time these young writers all showed promise. Who could know that Giraudoux was to outshine Morand? That François Mauriac would become universally known whereas Lucien Daudet, in spite of his famous name, would never capture the attention of the great public?

Lucien Daudet

Proust's acquaintance with Lucien Daudet stretched back before the turn of the century. The Daudet family was among the first to recognize Proust's genius. Alphonse and Mme Daudet had met him at the home of Mme Arthur Baignères when Proust was in his mid-twenties. They were taken by Proust's exquisite manners and asked Reynaldo Hahn, already an habitué of the Daudet house, to bring Proust with him to call. For Proust it was another dream come true. Daudet had been one of his favorite authors as a child, and to be received by the master seemed a great privilege. Read his reply to a dinner invitation: "Je ne peux pas vous dire, Monsieur, combien je suis touché de votre bonté. Mes plus beaux rêves quand j'étais enfant n'auraient rien pu me permettre d'aussi invraisemblable et d'aussi délicieux que d'être aussi gracieusement reçu un jour par le Maître qui m'inspirait déjà une admiration et un respect passionnés, dont je vous prie, etc. . . ." [14] He soon became a regular visitor at the Thursdays of the rue de Bellechasse. The Daudets welcomed him with great cordiality, even to the grandmother, who found Proust one of the most charming young men she had ever met. Lucien, the second son, then about fifteen and not always permitted to mingle with the guests, was most taken of all.

[13] *Correspondance générale*, III, 221.
[14] Lucien Daudet, *Autour De Soixante Lettres de Marcel Proust*, p. 13.

The best account of Proust's friendship with Lucien Daudet is told by Daudet himself in his essay preceding his selected letters. The sixty letters he presents are only a small part of those in his possession. About four hundred have never been made available. After a painful first visit to Proust's apartment in which the shy schoolboy floundered in his attempts at conversation, they grew more at ease with each other and became good friends and companions. Proust assumed the role of leader and guide. Together they went frequently to museums, galleries, and theaters, where Proust initiated his young disciple into the mysteries of art. Together they spent long hours talking of literature and society, Proust's major preoccupations. They were frequently joined by Proust's other companions: Reynaldo Hahn, Robert de Flers, Robert de Billy, Frédéric de Madrazo. These were happy years of comradeship. With Lucien, Proust became an adolescent again. Often in society they would have fits of giggles that would disgrace them both. Montesquiou was outraged at one of their attacks, but he had been particularly ill-disposed toward Lucien ever since the boy had inadvertently dropped a *chou praliné* in the count's top hat, one day when he was helping serve his mother's guests.

As Daudet moved into the orbit of the Empress Eugénie, he saw less and less of Proust. The Empress spent most of her time out of Paris. But whenever Daudet returned to the capital there were pleasant reunions. After the war, something of an estrangement darkened their friendship. Daudet was in Paris working in one of the war offices. But he found Proust changed and surrounded by new friends. Lucien, whom his elder brother referred to as the "aristocrate de la famille,"[15] felt that Proust had descended to the level of a professional writer. How pleased Proust was by such a "descent"!

The "professional writer," although hagridden by the labor his own publications entailed, gave generous thought to his friend's. He wrote to Jacques Rivière in 1920 that Daudet's *Evidences*[16] was possibly a chef-d'oeuvre and hoped that the *N. R. F.* might review it. Did he really believe it to be? Or is this just the gesture of a friend? His subsequent reference to the work sounds like faint praise: "Je ne sais pas pourquoi Lucien Daudet s'est mis à écrire à la mode d'aujourd'hui, mais vous verrez comme la ligne est tout de même plus ferme, plus large."[17] Daudet's novels reveal a delicate psychologist and a skillful word painter. He might have developed into an important writer if he had not sacrificed everything to follow the Empress Eugénie. It is disappointing not

[15] Léon Daudet, *Salons et journaux*, Chap. IX.
[16] *Marcel Proust et Jacques Rivière* (Plon, 1955), p. 131.
[17] *Ibid.*, p. 138.

to find as yet in Proust's letters more ample comments on Daudet's writing or appraisals of his talent.

Lucien's brother, Léon, seems never to have been the companion for Proust that Lucien was, although they were on the most cordial of terms and encountered each other often in society. Once, due to a chance meeting in a hotel at Fontainebleau, they spent an entire week together, strolling in the forest during the day and chatting by the fire in the evening. Léon Daudet recognized in Proust "un esprit de premier ordre, d'une culture infinie et dissimulée, ayant des vues originales sur tout." [18] During the years they exchanged courteous letters complimenting each other on their works, and it is Léon Daudet, one will recall, whose support won for Proust the Goncourt prize.

François Mauriac

Young François Mauriac was one of the guests at the reception the Daudets gave in honor of Jammes early in 1918. Although Proust's main attention was for Jammes, his eyes wandered frequently toward this new young writer, who was uncomfortably aware that he was being examined. When he saw that Proust was going to speak to him, his embarrassment increased in anticipation of the compliment he was about to receive. To his disappointment, Proust said only, "Francis Jammes vous a dédié une bien jolie nouvelle!" [19] a remark in which the novice author could see interest only in Jammes.

A word of approbation or praise from Proust would have delighted Mauriac. He had admired him from afar since, as a youth, he had first read the translation of Ruskin's *Sesame and Lilies.* The preface (reproduced in *Pastiches et mélanges* under the title *Une Journée de lecture*) had opened for him the door to a new world. Now, in the home of his friend Lucien Daudet, he was at last in the presence of this strange and fascinating genius: "Il m'apparut plutôt petit, cambré dans un habit très ajusté, les épais cheveux noirs ombrageant des pupilles dilatées, semblait-il, par les drogues. Engoncé dans un col très haut, le plastron bombé comme par un bréchet, il arrêta sur moi un œil de nocturne dont la fixité m'intimidait." [20]

Mauriac saw Proust only once more for any length of time, a few months before his death, one night when he was asked to dine by Proust's bedside. Between the first and the last meetings there had grown up a great mutual sympathy. Its rapid evolution can be followed in the dedications and letters which Mauriac has published in *Du Côté*

[18] "Des Lettres inédites de Marcel Proust," p. 3.
[19] Mauriac, *Du Côté de chez Proust* (La Table Ronde, 1947), p. 19.
[20] *Ibid.*, pp. 18-19.

de chez Proust. Proust writes Mauriac about his book, about Jammes, compliments the hopeful young writer on *Préséances* and *Genitrix.* At one point he makes a particularly interesting observation regarding the technique of the novel: "Cher ami, et ceci n'a pas un rapport direct avec ce que je viens de vous dire, je prise peu d'habitude le côté parlé des livres et j'y vois un manque de transposition." [21] In Proust's eyes, the simple recording of ordinary conversation cannot qualify as art. Elsewhere he will declare his disapproval of the "slice of life" technique.[22] These remarks anticipate the principles he will set forth in the last volume of his work where he speaks of the "fausseté même de l'art prétendu réaliste." [23]

Jean Cocteau

Marcel Proust became acquainted with Cocteau in 1911. The gifted nineteen-year-old was a friend of Robert and Lucien Daudet, and, like the others of the little coterie, paid faithful court to the ailing master. He repaid them by his marvelous conversation and his affectionate letters; he even let them read his work in manuscript. Cocteau volunteered to try to persuade Fasquelle to publish Proust's book, but without success. What impression his young admirer first made upon Proust is recorded in a letter to Robert de Billy: "Je m'étais lié avec un jeune poète très remarquablement intelligent et doué qui s'appelle M. Jean Cocteau. . . . Il est tout à fait gentil." [24] But his mischievous talent for caricature pushed him to a cruel description of Cocteau's appearance: "Car il a vraiment lui-même l'air d'une sirène avec son nez en fine arête de poisson, ses yeux fascinateurs. Et aussi l'air d'un hippocampe." [25] One gathers from subsequent comments that, in spite of his first enthusiasm, Proust was not particularly taken by the "figure parisienne et boulevardière" [26] of Cocteau. However, he saw him frequently and remained on very friendly terms with him.

Maurice Rostand

In trying to interest Fasquelle in *Swann,* Cocteau appealed to Maurice Rostand and his famous father to use their influence. Both held Proust in high esteem. Maurice was one of Cocteau's companions and shared the group's admiration for Proust. He sensed, however, far better than Cocteau, that behind Proust's great cordiality there were certain reserva-

[21] *Ibid.,* p. 30.
[22] See p. 103, n. 37.
[23] *Le Temps retrouvé,* II, 25. (See "Emile Zola," p. 71 of present work.)
[24] Billy, *Marcel Proust,* p. 72.
[25] *Correspondance générale,* V, 80.
[26] *Ibid.,* IV, 53.

tions. Both Proust and Cocteau tried to persuade him that he was wrong, but one suspects his intuition had not played him false. Proust was, of course, deeply grateful for Maurice's activity with Fasquelle on his behalf and for the praise heaped on his work.[27] Under the influence of his emotion he would even write that Rostand "a des dons étonnants de poète" and that he had always felt for him "de la sympathie . . . au lieu de l'antipathie qu'il s'imagine." [28] Yet he repeatedly refused to receive him, putting him off by such tricks as "une des lettres les plus chaleureuses que j'aie jamais écrites à quelqu'un." [29] A pen portrait he leaves of Rostand is as cruelly clever as the one of Cocteau. He is writing Gautier-Vignal of the visit of M. . . (presumably Maurice Rostand) while he was receiving another guest who was at the time greatly afflicted by a family sorrow: "Mais plus gai, plus rapide, plus ondoyant que jamais, il avait l'air dans les scènes tragiques de la pièce du Gymnase d'autrefois, de la visite froufroutante, gracieuse et intempestive de la dame élégante qui ne sait rien de ce qui se passe." [30] These two effeminate young men, Cocteau and Rostand, with their cosmetics and girlish ways, doubtless embarrassed Proust and irritated him, like relatives one cannot disown.

Jacques Rivière

The recent publication of the Proust-Rivière correspondence (1914, 1919-22) gives a vivid picture of one of Proust's last friendships. It is indeed a remarkable relationship, as Philip Kolb observes in his preface to the letters, based on a common devotion to literature, high regard one for the other, and a most unusual eagerness to be of service. Yet it is not a model friendship, serene and wholly beautiful, for self-interest and neurosis are too conspicuously present. As we read the letters exchanged between the irascible writer and the meek, conciliatory editor, we unfortunately recall an earlier correspondence between the young Proust and Robert de Montesquiou. Now Proust is the *grand seigneur* who overwhelms with abuse or affection depending upon his mood. Only his illness and his understandable anxiety over his life's labor—so little time and so little strength remain to him—can excuse Proust's sarcasm, insinuations, and complaints. Only Rivière's genuine admiration, his physical lassitude, and his concern for the interests of the *Nouvelle Revue Française* can explain his sweet patience. But if less lovely than one might hope for these two dedicated spirits who have not long to live, realization

[27] See Rostand's article, "Quelques Lignes sur un livre unique," *Comoedia*, December 26, 1913. Proust speaks of the "ridicule exagération" of its praise of *Swann*. *Marcel Proust et Jacques Rivière*, p. 19.

[28] Robert, *Comment Débuta Marcel Proust*, p. 37.

[29] *Ibid.*, p. 60.

[30] *Correspondance générale*, III, 320.

of the issues at stake and the nightmare of physical and mental suffering the two were enduring makes the dialogue represented by their letters all the more poignant and human.

Without questioning the mutual gestures of affection and esteem lavished in these letters, one may nonetheless suppose, behind the blandishments and politeness, a good measure of self-interest on both sides. At the beginning, if Proust responded warmly to Rivière's advances, it is because his work was involved. Rivière's praise for *Swann* touched its author deeply. But for Proust, Rivière was not only a very perceptive critic capable of divining the deep intentions of a work, he was also the secretary of the N. R. F., the review and publishing house that Proust still hankered after. The N. R. F., for its part, was very eager to obtain the collaboration of this writer whose work, although it once had rejected it, now appeared to be a great literary event. The circumstances of Gide's letter of apology to Proust suggest, as we have already observed,[31] a concerted effort to woo Proust to the organization. One remembers the story. When the novel appeared in November, 1913, it was given to Henri Ghéon for review. After reading it, Ghéon urged it upon Rivière "avec empressement, insistance et chaleur." Rivière, in turn, passed it enthusiastically to Gide. Gide, likewise smitten by the work, wrote to Proust to tell him so and apologize for having previously rejected it.[32] If these be the facts of the matter, one may wonder at Ghéon's article in the January issue of the *N.R.F.*, which has the tone more of the former *N.R.F.* prejudice than of the new enthusiasm. One might suspect the change of heart there came after the article was written, due possibly to the growing attention the book was obtaining elsewhere in the press. But before the time of Gide's letter in January, its fame was not yet considerable or significant enough to make this suspicion very plausible. Moreover, Gide and his group were notoriously independent spirits. It seems difficult to doubt, therefore, that the very cordial letters from the *N.R.F.* that suddenly rained upon Proust were motivated by sincerest admiration for his work. After Gide's letter, there was Rivière's, and also one from Gaston Gallimard. Ghéon, to whom Proust had written indignantly about his review, sent a highly soothing reply. But sincere admiration does not mean disinterestedness. They all wished to repair an unfortunate blunder, and claim this writer of whose genius they were now convinced as their very own.

Gide's second letter to Proust is an invitation to leave his publisher Grasset and come in with them. Proust regretfully declined. Whereupon Gide asked to publish extracts of the forthcoming second volume in the

[31] See p. 82 ff.
[32] See p. 83, n. 78.

Nouvelle Revue Française. Jacques Rivière seconded the request. His collaboration once obtained, the *N. R. F.* would henceforth make countless concessions, go to infinite pains, wheedle and cajole to keep in their midst the great novelist. The responsibility was chiefly on Rivière's shoulders. His apologies, humility, and solicitous concern for Proust's health were doubtless sincere. But he would push as much as he dared to obtain copy from Proust. "Vraiment, vraiment, ne vous sentez-vous pas au bout de la plume un petit article sur Sainte-Beuve, par exemple? Il ferait merveille dans mon numéro d'avril." [33] Without waiting for a reply, he sent off the *Lundis* to Proust, "pour le cas où l'envie vous viendrait de les ouvrir." Time after time he alluded delicately but insistently to the subject. How ironical that all the while Proust had a voluminous essay on Sainte-Beuve among his papers! Proust, as one might expect, was gratified to be plagued by such a gadfly. But he was no dupe. He knew Rivière's devotion to the review. He could grumble that Rivière never did anything he considered—rightly or wrongly—against its best interests, such as accepting contributions from some of the "gens de grand talent" whom Proust recommended.[34] Proust, on the other hand, knew his own worth to the magazine and felt free to be as temperamental as he liked. If he stayed with the *N. R. F.* it was not merely to please Jacques Rivière. It was because the only proper setting for a work such as his was the house of Gallimard.

This being said, there still remains mutual admiration and fondness. Proust's work must indeed have exercised great appeal for Jacques Rivière, a person of keen literary sensibilities and a taste for psychological analysis. He possessed the qualities of an ideal reader of Proust. The comments and criticism that accompany his praise of each new piece of *À La Recherche du temps perdu* as it appeared, contain some very just observations. More astute than Ghéon, who found *Swann* exactly the opposite of a work of art, from the first Rivière discerned evidence of a composition which, although unorthodox and not readily apparent, nevertheless existed. Proust's delight in Rivière's perspicacity prompted him to make some illuminating confidences. He abhors, as he explains, the sort of book in which an author declares his intentions too conspicuously. He finds it "plus probe et plus délicat" not to announce that the object of his novel is the pursuit of truth or what the nature of that truth is for him. Deliberately creating false impressions, he will withhold correcting them until the end of his novel. He indignantly refutes Ghéon's assertion that his book is just an assembly of souvenirs, on the

[33] *Marcel Proust et Jacques Rivière,* p. 86.

[34] Lacretelle, "Un Témoignage sur Proust," pp. 13-14. See also *Bulletin de la Société des Amis de Marcel Proust,* III (1953), 20.

grounds that, ill as he is, he would never carry on were it not for a compelling mission. If he chooses to present the evolution of a thought by means of fiction rather than the essay, it is to make it the more living. Letter I in the Proust-Rivière collection is interesting evidence of Proust's aim and technique in writing *À La Recherche du temps perdu.* Letter LXIV offers another curious and valuable piece of enlightenment. Rivière had written that he found *Guermantes I* more poetic than psychological, lacking sustained psychological developments such as the quarrel with Gilberte or the crystallization of Marcel's love for Albertine. Proust replied:

> J'ajoute un postscriptum à ma lettre pour vous remercier et vous rassurer au sujet du côté "psychologique de mon œuvre." Comme elle est une construction, forcément, il y a des pleins, des piliers, et dans l'intervalle des 2 piliers je peux me livrer aux minutieuses peintures. Tout le volume sur la séparation d'avec Albertine, sa mort, l'oubli, laisse loin derrière lui la brouille avec Gilberte. De sorte qu'il y aura trois esquisses très différentes du même sujet (séparation de Swann avec Odette dans *Un amour de Swann*—brouille avec Gilberte dans les *Jeunes Filles en fleurs*—séparation avec Albertine dans *Sodome et Gomorrhe,* la meilleure partie).[35]

Although Proust lavished the same sort of attention upon all his friends, Rivière must have been sincerely touched by Proust's many personal attentions. Rivière's last years were hard ones. His health already undermined, he returned from the war to assume responsibilities that could only make it worse. Harassed by his duties as editor, preoccupied by his personal life and his family, worried about his financial situation, Rivière's strength gradually ebbed away. Proust recommended doctors to him and politely took care of the bill, lent him money and aided him, by pushing prizes and lectures his way, to earn more himself. The great invalid Proust did his best to succor a fellow sufferer, and the letters from these two men who were soon to die are full of touching solicitude one for the other, and mutual comfort.

It is difficult to evaluate Proust's praise for Rivière the writer. Except for minor restrictions (a device well known to Proust as a means of enhancing the compliment), he speaks highly of everything. What he has to say about *Aimée* read only in manuscript is insignificant, limited to flattering phrases and some stylistic corrections, the majority of which Rivière will not choose to follow. Racing against death to finish his own work, Proust could not seriously devote himself to another's. Without his encouragement and praise, however, *Aimée* would probably never have appeared.

Jacques Rivière, whose role in life seems to have been that of a disciple,

[35] *Marcel Proust et Jacques Rivière,* p. 114.

had found, after Gide and Claudel, a master in Proust. Being one of the first to recognize his genius and associating it with the *N. R. F.* must have been one of his greatest gratifications. Proust had found in Rivière, besides a disciple and editor, a man whom he could place "au plus haut de mon estime intellectuelle et morale." [36] Their friendship was an exceedingly fruitful one, for themselves (as each served his own interests best by serving the other's), and for the glory of French literature.

Jacques Chardonne and Jacques de Lacretelle

In manuals of literature, Jacques Rivière's novel is usually grouped with those of Jacques Chardonne and Jacques de Lacretelle, also *moralistes* and painters of sentiment in the French tradition that stems from *La Princesse de Clèves.* Neither Chardonne nor Lacretelle escaped the attention of Proust who, while his own career was about to close, watched with curiosity those just beginning. Toward Chardonne he is outspokenly severe, writing to Jacques Boulenger apropos of *L'Epithalame*: "Quel battage! Ah! les 'tranches de vie,' quelle naïve erreur de principe, que beaucoup de talent suffirait à réduire." [37] It is true that Chardonne created many scenes drawn from life with fine precision, but to dismiss this delicate psychologist as just a misguided Realist is an injustice, which, happily, Boulenger did not let pass.

Jacques de Lacretelle, on the contrary, found favor with Proust, who praised *La Vie inquiète de Jean Hermelin* to the skies. On Proust's recommendation the book was reviewed in the *Nouvelle Revue Française.* Through his efforts, too, Lacretelle was himself invited to contribute to the magazine. He did a number of reviews for it and had the good fortune to publish in its pages two large extracts from his book *Silbermann,* subsequently published by the N. R. F.

When it was a question of the Goncourt prize, Proust preferred Lacretelle to Louis Chadourne. He frankly explains his attitude in a letter to Lacretelle himself. If Giraudoux had any chance of being chosen, Proust would be for him. But since he had not, Proust's support would go to Lacretelle, "le romancier d'avenir, le grand psychologue." [38] As for Chadourne, in spite of the latter's praise for Proust's work, Proust cannot reciprocate. *Inquiète Adolescence* "est à mon avis fort inférieur au vôtre." [39] Léon Daudet, Proust's powerful friend on the jury, did not

[36] *Correspondance générale,* III, 308.

[37] *Ibid.,* p. 280.

[38] "Un Témoignage sur Proust," p. 15. (In the same letter Proust assures Lacretelle that he does not know Giraudoux. According to Porel's testimony [p. 94, n. 11], Giraudoux called on him in 1919, that is, a year before the present letter.)

[39] *Ibid.,* p. 15.

share his enthusiasm. In fact, he found "le livre du petit Lacretelle idiot."[40]

Lacretelle called often at the apartment, 44 rue Hamelin, where Proust, mortally ill and beset by the problems of his own publication, nevertheless found time and strength to receive his young friends. In an address commemorating the thirtieth anniversary of Proust's death, Lacretelle recalls one of his visits, perhaps his last. He found Proust, either from fever or from drugs, "en proie à une merveilleuse exaltation poétique." He spoke of Gérard de Nerval and quoted from the *Chimères*. As Lacretelle departed and went out into the night, he tells us, "il me parut que Nerval et lui s'étaient unis pour me donner la clef de son œuvre."[41]

Our information concerning Proust's relations with writers of the 1920 generation is still far from ample. We may expect it to be greatly increased as his letters continue to appear. However, enough exists to let us marvel that this writer, hastening to finish his own work before taking leave both of literature and of life, could have such genuine interest in those just coming in. He cultivated their acquaintance and encouraged them in their efforts. His praise often seems to exceed his real sentiments and his encouragement is offset by some disparagement. But allowing for his personal quirks and his state of health, Proust's attitude toward his juniors is generous and patiently paternal, completely free from condescension or patronage. Moreover, his advice seems generally sound and his judgments, if not all sustained by posterity, indicate a subtlety of critical appreciation that makes them worthy of note.

[40] *Ibid.*, p. 17.

[41] "Allocution de M. Jacques de Lacretelle," *Bulletin de la Société des Amis de Marcel Proust*, IV (1954), 35.

CHAPTER FIVE

Conclusion

Collecting Proust's observations on his contemporaries has been, as anticipated, rather like an interview with Proust himself. Fragmentary and often not to be taken at face value, like remarks made in conversation, they give just glimpses, but very precious ones, not only of the authors in question but of Proust too. Through personal letters, diaries, and verbatim reports, we have gathered interesting bits of the intimate story of his life and spiritual development. It is as if he were telling from his own lips of his boyhood, when he joined his schoolfellows to discuss the literary heroes of the hour and plan the reviews to which his first critical efforts would be dedicated; of his young manhood, when he met the literary fashionables in Parisian drawing rooms; of his invalid years, when his own work took shape, and letters and callers were his chief contacts with the literary world; of the years of triumph that preceded his death when, from the perspective of a lifetime, he surveyed the current developments and tendencies in literature and formulated his final views on questions of esthetics. We have heard him, at each stage in his life, talk about his friends, about their work and about its meaning for him; we have noted what he learned from this writer and that one, and have observed his talent develop and his concept of literature in the process of formation. As he talked about others, we have watched him for disclosures he would make about himself, for his comments on others have been like a mirror held before his own face.

A chat, I suggested, with a gentleman of exquisite culture and sensitivity. Nowhere has Proust shown more clearly the subtlety of his perception than in dealing with the work of another writer. He discovers qualities and affinities, exposes flaws that would escape all but the most acute of readers. Moreover, he is an extremely mannered and quaintly polite gentleman, whose refined observations are expressed in a language equally refined. His words take us back to old-fashioned drawing rooms where persons of distinction would vie with one another in inventing pretty compliments and witty retorts. As we read them, the murmur of politics, parlor intrigues, jealousies, and ambitions can clearly be heard like tea-party chitchat. Against this background Proust and his friends come back to life and take up again their social and literary careers.

The writers Proust discusses could not possibly possess for him the abstractness and pure aloofness of figures of literary history: they were living contemporaries, for the most part his friends. Knowing a writer as a person complicates one's judgments. As Proust wrote to Robert Dreyfus: "Peut-être y a-t-il des choses qui font un peu rire parce que nous connaissons l'auteur, ce qui n'implique pas une faute littéraire, et ce que la postérité ignorera. Mérimée ou Jacquemont riaient quelquefois de choses de Stendhal et avaient tort. . . ." [1] But we are grateful for the eyewitness account. If it almost precludes an impersonal estimation, it lends to whatever is said a living warmth and the intimate quality of conversation, which possess for us quite as much utility and far more charm. In a time when criticism, at least in America, is self-conscious about looking beyond the work of art itself, it is important to reaffirm the value of corollary studies. M. André Billy reminds us in *L'Epoque 1900:* "L'histoire littéraire est froide parce que, uniquement livresque, elle oublie que la littérature est une chose vivante, elle néglige . . . les écrivains en tant qu'hommes, elle ramène tout à des textes. . . . Il serait bon de réagir contre le préjugé en vertu duquel les œuvres comptent seules." [2] I shall feel thoroughly gratified if in this study Proust and his subjects of criticism have emerged as living persons.

In the preface to his translation of the *Bible of Amiens,* Proust defines the function of a critic:

> Au fond, aider le lecteur à être impressionné par ces traits singuliers, placer sous ses yeux des traits similaires qui lui permettent de les tenir pour les traits essentiels du génie d'un écrivain devrait être la première partie de la tâche de tout critique.
>
> S'il a senti cela, et aidé les autres à le sentir, son office est à peu près rempli. Et, s'il ne l'a pas senti, il pourra écrire tous les livres du monde sur . . . "l'homme, l'écrivain, le prophète, l'artiste, la portée de son action, les erreurs de la doctrine," toutes ces constructions s'élèveront peut-être très haut, mais à côté du sujet: elles pourront porter aux nues la situation littéraire du critique, mais ne vaudront pas, pour l'intelligence de l'œuvre, la perception exacte d'une nuance juste, si légère semble-t-elle.
>
> Je conçois pourtant que le critique devrait ensuite aller plus loin. Il essayerait de reconstituer ce que pouvait être la singulière vie spirituelle d'un écrivain hanté de réalitées si spéciales, son inspiration étant la mesure dans laquelle il avait la vision de ces réalités, son talent la mesure dans laquelle il pouvait les recréer dans son œuvre, sa moralité enfin, l'instinct qui les lui faisant considérer sous un aspect d'éternité (quelque particulières que ces réalités nous paraissent) le poussait à sacrifier au besoin de les apercevoir et à la nécessité de les reproduire pour en assurer une vision durable et claire, tous ses plaisirs, tous ses devoirs et jusqu'à sa propre vie, laquelle n'avait de raison d'être que comme étant la seule manière possible d'entrer en contact avec ces réalités, de valeur

[1] Dreyfus, *Souvenirs sur Marcel Proust,* p. 217.
[2] P. 5.

que celle que peut avoir pour un physicien un instrument indispensable à ses expériences.[3]

How does a critic determine or "feel" the essential traits of an author? Proust does not explicitly tell us here, but interpreting his words from his general attitude in psychological and esthetic matters, we may reasonably assume that he considers the process quite subjective in nature. Factors in the critic's own personality will play a large part in guiding his choice. He will note particularly the features that interest him, feel deeply the qualities toward which by temperament or experience he is already disposed. This type of criticism, the essential and indispensable one according to Proust, implies a communion or collaboration between author and critic. The critic, in selecting what he finds outstanding in an author, draws in some of his own features. Thus the picture he passes on to the public is unmistakably his and necessarily different from the one the reader has previously seen and different from the one that the next critic will present.

The authors we have been viewing through Proust's eyes have now for us the countenance they had for Proust. Our concept of them has been more or less altered. And in proportion as we have gained new insights concerning them, we have gained new insights concerning Proust. We may question the validity of the former—in the light of previous impressions, we may reject Proust's picture—but we can be sure his interpretation of an author is a true reflection of his own personality.

We see behind Proust's remarks the proof of his profound and exclusive dedication to art. Art was for him the way of life, the goal of life, the meaning of life. At a time like the present when "engagement" and preoccupation with "social significance" threaten to turn artists from their primary mission, it is well to meditate the example of Proust.

Thus the Anatole France of Marcel Proust was above all a stylist. He was the writer of elegant and harmonious prose, full of delicate mannerisms and civilized irony. The thinker, the scholar, the social historian, were not the France that Proust saw first. Proust's love of art disposed him to forgive much in Montesquiou and grant him a far greater place in literature than history has assigned him. Anna de Noailles was for Proust the happy combination of a beautiful person and a creator of beauty. His use of the word beauty in connection with her writing is so frequent and insistent that it has necessitated a particular definition. He discussed only slightly Barrès's political ideas and the philosophy expressed in his work, but rejoiced in the evocativeness of his pen and his masterly handling of language. The opulent and ironic manner of Henri de Régnier found greater favor in Proust's eyes than it enjoys today, when

[3] Reproduced in *Pastiches et mélanges*, pp. 108-9.

writers feel they have more to do than to describe decaying châteaux and futile and whimsical lives.

Proust's attention to his friends and classmates has given us a picture of writers we might otherwise not have seen at all. Dreyfus, Halévy, Robert were but names to most of us. Others such as Gregh, Vaudoyer, and Boylesve have acquired interesting detail. Some writers whose features we are wont to admire may have lost, now that Proust has pointed out their shortcomings, some of their beauty or significance. Péguy, in particular, receives no embellishment from the hands of our critic. Writers of the next generation—Cocteau, Giraudoux, Mauriac, and Morand—whose features fame has cast for us in a permanent mold, become again, as we read Proust, callow young artists of uncertain character and orientation. The Nobel Prize winner of 1952 has become a young man anxious for praise and encouragement from an elder.

In his analysis Proust affirms that the critic should delve even deeper, should try to indicate behind the essential traits the spiritual life of his subject. Has not Proust done so in describing the joyous natural world of Francis Jammes, the splendid universe of Régnier and Noailles, the vision of life in Robert's *Roman d'un malade*, and Maeterlinck's thoughts on death? An artist's work should be, Proust declares, the record of his spiritual life. He emphasizes the seriousness of his own mission, the devotion and sacrifice even of his life, to reading and recording the fundamental realities that are disclosed to him. Everywhere that Proust has discussed writers may be found allusions to the greatness of their task and the nature of true art. They constitute an enlightening amplification of the philosophy of art enunciated in *Le Temps retrouvé*.

Proust states repeatedly that it is an artist's vision that is all-important. With France, Noailles, Barrès, and Dreyfus he asserts that the quality of great art is to convey a new glimpse of the world, the particular one of the artist. It has no other aims. No didacticism, no "engagement," no theory must distract the writer from his essential function. The objective and scientific aspirations of Realism are denounced as trivial or futile. Documentation or enumeration can never produce the true aspect of reality. Only by means of the metaphor, the "inevitable" metaphor, in which a hidden analogy is discovered between disparate objects or phenomena, can an artist disclose the real nature of things. Although in recording his vision the artist faces an arduous task demanding all his skill, technique or craftsmanship is only of secondary importance. And correctness and propriety of language are questionable virtues, for each artist must recreate his language, fashion it into the medium best suited to his inspiration. The product of true art is beauty, but it is the beauty of revealed truth, the faithful record of the inner experience of the artist. What

Proust alludes to briefly in defining the critic's role, concerning the artist's function, he has amply developed through his own criticism.

Following the passage above, in which Proust defines the critic's highest function as an attempt to determine the spiritual life of an author, his particular vision of reality, he modestly adds that his own ambition in this little essay on Ruskin does not aim so high: "cette petite étude qui aura comblé mes ambitions si elle donne le désir de lire Ruskin et de revoir quelques cathédrales."

At the risk of being presumptuous, I hope that this study of Proust and his contemporaries has contributed to our knowledge of Proust's "special realities" and "spiritual life." I hope, too, that it has "given the desire" to reread some of the authors discussed, and revisit, even though they may be a bit out of our way, some of the literary monuments of the early years in our century.

Index of Names Cited